Angel

MW00917606

I Dated The Devil And His Brother

Angelina Taylor

Dedication Page

Dedicated to Kristin

I call this my book, but it is really several pieces of wisdom woven from lunches, dinners, and walks with this wise sage. Kristin, thank you for every tear you captured and every word you heard me speak. Thank you for your love and patience. Thank you for being the instrument God used to help me to grow emotionally.

Dedicated to My All-Stars—My Sister Friends

You will be reading a book from a seemingly put together woman, but I am who I am because of the love and prayers of so many people who have prayed me through the worst of times. I am grateful for all of you.

ISBN: 978-1-725-80115-8

Cover Design by: Morgan Jones

Bible Copyright Notices

Table of Contents

Chapter 1

The Beginning Before the Beginning

About two years ago I had an idea to write a book called "I Dated the Devil and His Brother," and the Lord clearly did NOT give His stamp of approval. If you are spiritually in tune, you know when you are desiring to do something that is out of the will of God. In addition, there are times that you may want to do something, but it isn't time yet. When I thought about writing this book, I kept hearing NO in my spirit but the title never left me. It wasn't until recently that I didn't ask but instead heard in my spirit that now is the time to write the book.

Now before you think that this is a male bashing book, it is not. It is my story about looking for love in all the wrong places and realizing that God was standing here all along waiting for me to choose Him and receive love from Him. It isn't about men being devils and women being angels. It is the story of choosing to be led astray and the redemptive love of God drawing us back to the place He had for us all along. This is a book dedicated to brokenhearted people who are wondering will love ever find them. Love has found you. Will you receive it?

The Beginning

Wouldn't it be nice if I could say that I'm going to present to you stories of love gone wrong? But in reality these are not love stories at all. These are stories of relationships that should have never been. If we were using the type of love described in I Corinthians 13, then we could compare the type of love that may have ultimately hurt us to agape love. Agape is a Greek word meaning unconditional love. It is the kind of love that means I will love you through thick and thin, and dare I say I mean no harm to you as I love you through life.

When a relationship ends, we may wonder if agape love was ever present. If it was, would we end up so hurt? Instead the stories in this book were derived from a need to be loved but choosing to receive love from the wrong people. This is where my journey to find love began.

I had been divorced for about three years and was thinking about moving forward. I had been on a few dates, but I hadn't found what I was looking for. Don't ask what that is because I'm still trying to figure it out. But what I knew is that the men I was meeting were not for me. And then he appeared.

I met him in an unexpected place and knew instantly there was something about him that I really liked.

This man that I shall call Adam was working as a substitute teacher at my school, and after school we would talk about the challenges of transitioning from the military to teaching. He was pleasant and kind, and my heart fluttered every time he was near. Did I mention that his daughter just happened to be in my class?

Now my instinct was to NOT get involved because surely these were two obstacles to keeping my professional and personal life separate. But the third obstacle is what should have made me run to the nearest exit. In one of our conversations he said that he was substitute teaching because if he didn't work he would be at home drinking. A more intellectually savvy woman would have said to herself that this man is telling me that he has a problem with drinking, but not me. All I felt were heart flutters and followed those flutters into what would be my darkest abyss. In the early days of us connecting, I discussed our relationship with my pastor when I saw him at a book signing. I was purchasing a book on marriage, and he asked if the book was for me. I told him it was for a friend, and he asked if I was thinking about getting married again. I told him about the man I was interested in, and he pointed out another red flag. We were unequally yoked. Adam grew up in a different faith but had walked away from that faith years ago. At this point in his life he was bordering on being agnostic, which should have been another reason I ran in the opposite direction. But unfortunately, I went in the direction where my heart was fluttering.

And so it began. First it was talking after school, and then there was the invitation to go on a date. I think Adam and I might have laughed and said that it wasn't a date, him being a widower and me being apprehensive, but we both dove in anyway. And the date was wonderful. Adam was wonderful. He was everything I had been looking for since recovering from my divorce.

Our dates were always fun, and I enjoyed spending time with him and his daughters. I didn't feel any pressure to be a surrogate mother, and everything was great. I remember being at his house for dinner, and he drank with dinner but nothing too alarming. But there were other dinners that I noticed he was drinking more than I was comfortable with. I told myself that maybe it was okay because he was at home, and he really wasn't a mean drunk. I'm just overreacting, right?

Until the first time he called me drunk and slurring his words. I had never known that type of heartbreak until that moment. The heartbreak of loving someone who was slowly destroying himself. What I would come to learn is that this relationship would compound heartbreak after heartbreak the longer I stayed connected with him. Back to that night…that pivotal moment in our relationship. Adam not only called me and had a long and sad conversation with me, but the next day when I got the courage to say how much I disliked the phone call he couldn't remember any of it.

Over time I watched Adam drink and drink and drink to the point that his daughters would call me looking for him, but all of us knew where he was. He was at a local bar drinking his sorrows away. What I saw initially as a wonderful, sweet man was only a façade for the sad man he really was. As I got to know him and the internal wounds he carried, I understood the drinking. Did that make me an enabler? Probably. I never came over with beer in my hand to feed his demons, but I did stay with him for three years slowly dying inside from grief and sadness.

The worst night for me in those three years was the night he appeared on my doorstep inebriated beyond comprehension. I lived far from his local watering hole, and he somehow (I know now by the grace of God) arrived safely at my home. When I saw him, he had that sad look in his eyes but a smile that said take me in and show me love. My heart broke as he stumbled inside barely able to speak coherently and not able to answer any of the questions I had as to how he had gotten here. Not how he had gotten here physically but how had he gotten to this emotional place of brokenness that made him drink so much. I was both sad for him and afraid for him. All I could see at this point was his own self-destruction, yet all I did was stand idly by and watch the approaching train wreck. At least for a time I thought all I could do is watch. In the background of this relationship was someone else whom I looked up to spiritually. She had been saved a lot longer than I had, and she was encouraging me to stand strong and believe that God was going to deliver Adam from alcohol. She had me praying, laying hands, and fasting on his behalf. Because I was new in my faith, I didn't realize that I was out of order. God had never approved of this relationship. In fact God was sending red flags at almost every turn that said get out of this relationship. Save yourself and your sanity. I was trying to have a relationship with God and with a man tormented with demons and wondering why I felt so sad and defeated all the time.

I loved Adam. My heart both grieved for him and hoped beyond hope that he would get well so that we could have the relationship I wanted. Key words: the relationship that I wanted. He was a widower, so he never made any promises of a future or wanting anything more than a casual relationship. We spent time together and exchanged words of affection but never any discussion of something long term. I was still afraid of getting married again, and he wasn't in a place emotionally to want that level of commitment after the death of his wife. But we stayed together, and I still secretly hoped that we could make it work.

At this point this story already looks like it was heading for a tragic end, but there is another layer that made it more tragic. I became angry with God. Deeply angry. I was still going to church and serving in ministry. I was still somewhat nice to people on the surface, but underneath was a heart that was seething with anger at this situation. As I was growing in my faith, I was like a babe in Christ believing that God could do anything. Hadn't the saints told me that God would give me the desires of my heart? "Delight yourself in the Lord, and He shall give you the desires of your heart." (Psalm 37:4) Hindsight has shown me that I wasn't delighting myself in the Lord. I was delighting in Adam. I had made him my everything, and I desperately wanted the relationship to work. I thought that all God had to do was to do a miracle and set Adam free from alcohol. I was going to church and hearing sermons about people who had been delivered from drugs and alcohol, so I knew it was possible. Why hadn't God done it for Adam?

Let's be real. I didn't really want Adam to be free from alcohol for Adam or even his daughters. I wanted him to be set free for me so that I could have the fairy tale relationship that I thought would validate me after the divorce. I was praying and praying and praying, and God was silent. The more silent God was, the angrier I got. So guess what I did? I prayed louder and longer! Isn't that what we sometimes do? We think a begging prayer will move God to do our will. Our will and not His. My prayer warrior friend would come over and we would pray together on behalf of Adam because she had convinced me that "For where two or three are gathered together in My name, I am there in the midst of them." (Matthew 18:20) Again because I was following her lead, I didn't understand the depths of the word of God. I thought because I wanted something (or someone) I could pray this prayer and God was going to answer. So I kept praying, God kept silent, and I felt defeated.

How did all of this come to an end? After three years of loving Adam, Adam called me on a spring Sunday and said it was over. To paraphrase him the best I can, the phone call went like this. "I've been drinking about half of my life, and I'm not going to change." After those words I didn't hear anything else. I heard that this man was leaving me for alcohol, and this pivotal moment changed my life.

Chapter 2

The Interlude

How do you recover from heartbreak? Initially I didn't recover. I went to work the next day with tears in my eyes and immediately went to my friend's classroom and told her I needed her shoulder over the coming days and weeks. I walked around more numb than sad. And anger? There was no more anger with God. Now I was raging with anger towards Adam. How dare he leave me?!! ME!!! I was the good woman in this situation. Surely I was faultless and had only tried to love him. First of all, I need to take several seats on this one. The best advice I ever heard was when a pastor said that you cannot be a good woman to a man who doesn't want a good woman. Amen! Where was this priceless advice when I was choosing all the wrong men? (It was in my spirit all along, but I wasn't listening or obeying.) But again, Adam really wasn't the bad guy in this, nor was I a so-called "good woman." I was a selfish woman who was so desperate for love that I wanted to prop up a broken man, put him in a picture perfect relationship that I painted in my own mind, and God said no.

During this time my pastor was preaching a new series and had even traveled to London to preach the message. Must be pretty important, right? I can't tell you the title of the sermon, but I can tell you what the central verses were from the sermon. "And seeing from afar a fig tree having leaves, He went to see if perhaps He would find something on it. When He came to it, He found nothing but leaves, for it was not the season for figs. In response Jesus said to it, 'Let no one eat fruit from you ever again.'" (Mark 11:13-14) It was this story of the cursed fig tree that became the catalyst for my healing.

Jesus was coming out of Bethany, and he was hungry. Seeing the fig tree from afar He observed that the tree was producing no fruit, and as a result he cursed the tree from the root. I recognized in my own life that not only was that relationship producing no fruit in me, it was drying me up spiritually and emotionally. If Adam had not called me to break it off, who knows how much longer I would have stayed and what kind of condition I would have been in by the termination of the relationship. God saw fit to remove me from a cursed situation because I would have stayed there drying up and dying slowly.

Within just a few months two friends invited me to the Woman Thou Art Loosed! Conference, and one of them blessed me with the devotional Bible that goes along with the series. Immediately after the conference I began a year long study of the Bible and eventually added a study Bible and a few trusted commentaries to my study time. I even had a set time that I established to meet with God quietly and privately. I needed that time. Although I began this Bible study tattered and torn, eventually spending that time growing and getting to know God better brought me to a place of wholeness. To the person who is reading this and is brokenhearted, I can assure you that God is a healer. I was incredibly broken and shattered into a million pieces, but over time God put every piece back together and made me happy and whole. I felt a glow within me that could have only come from spending that time in the presence of God and allowing Him to heal every broken place.

The next step to healing was forgiving and releasing Adam, but it was not easy. In the early months of my quiet time with God, I had made a fire in my fireplace, and I was reading and studying in front of the fire. I was beginning to feel a sense of peace and joy. This is great, right? Except when I heard God telling me to pray for Adam, and I said no. Yes, I told the almighty God I was not going to pray for the person who had hurt me more than anyone ever. I know that in the Bible there are times that God repeats instructions, but this was more like a command. Pray for Adam. A second time I said no, to which God told me to stop reading and studying since I was being defiant and disobedient. And with pride and hurt, I closed my Bible and went to bed. I wish I could remember how long it took me to obey, but I'm guessing it was only a day or two. Not only did I pray for Adam, but I wrote him a letter forgiving and releasing him. In the almost two-page letter I thanked him for being the one who broke off the relationship and ultimately setting me free. I was in such turmoil during most of those three years that when it was over, I really could thank him and let him know I wished him all of the best.

After I wrote the letter there came a day that I was completely healed and whole. It was a bright spring day, and I was on my way out of the house. It was then that I not only felt sunshine on my face, but I felt as if light was finally shining through me. It was my breakthrough, and there I remained spiritually, emotionally, and mentally whole for seven years.

For seven years I was happy with just me and God. I was happy serving in ministry and growing professionally. I had too much going on in my life to worry about having a relationship. Hindsight tells me I should have stayed in that place, but then there would very possibly be no story to tell or book to write.

Chapter 3

The Story in Between

If you have ever studied the book of Genesis and the story of Joseph, you know that there is an insertion of a story that seems out of place. It is the story of Tamar. I often wondered why the writer of the book, even under the guidance of the Holy Spirit, would drop such a strange story in the middle of Joseph's story. Tamar's story seems to have nothing to do with Joseph's story. In fact Tamar's story is a sordid tale that seems far too steamy to be in the pages of the Bible. It's one that preachers may approach warily if there are children in the room. Why would God include a story like the one found in Genesis 38?

In studying this chapter and reading various commentaries, the story reminds me of the ones I hear from people who are honest about their struggles with the flesh. Judah was the patriarch of the family, and Tamar was his daughter in law. In Jewish tradition, when a man dies his brother is supposed to produce children with her to continue the family line. I will spare you the gory details that I encourage you to read in Genesis 38, but Judah's sons did not fulfill their responsibility so Tamar came up with another plan. Isn't that what we do when things don't pan out the way we think they should? We go our own way and often that turns out disastrous.

The story in Genesis 38 begins with Judah making some poor decisions. Instead of spending time with his own people, he left the tribe to cavort with the women of Canaan. As a result of making this decision early on, he opened himself up to be seduced by Tamar later when she disguised herself as a prostitute so that she could get pregnant and produce the child she knew she was intended to have. Interestingly enough Chapters 37 and 39 are about Joseph, a type of Christ and what most Bible scholars would consider a good and godly man. But Jesus doesn't come from the lineage of Joseph. He came from the line of Judah, indicating the redemptive power of God.

The next story you are about to read came about as a result of me sharing my own story with several people. My sharing gave other women the willingness to share their own stories. I submit to you another sordid tale.

The Story – Submitted by Anonymous

We are lying in bed discussing his upcoming trip out of town and how much he is going to miss me. He came over early to make sure that he had the chance to see me before everything else he had to do today.

He also had to come over when the "coast was clear" because he was a married man…and the upcoming trip was his honeymoon. How did I get here you might ask? Well, it's a long and stupid story that if I didn't live it, I wouldn't believe it myself.

I met Duncan 8 years ago at work. He was handsome, sexy, and we flirted immediately. It was not until a month or so later that I discovered one of my friends also wanted him. Too late, we were already sexually involved and she was not his type. In my head, I had won because he was mine. In reality, I was being set up to lose in a major way.

Since this is a tale about married men and how they live secret lives and not about a foolish woman like myself and all of her angst about being alone, wanting companionship, someone to love her and ultimately validate her as a human being; I'll quickly rush through the years of dating before our pre-honeymoon romp.

Things started out fairly well, we went on a date. A date, yes I said a single, solitary date to a nice restaurant and then we started having what I affectionately call "house dates." He came over to my place or I went over to his. I met one of his children, he met both of mine. We hung out and had sex. Oh we talked daily about some really interesting things. Our friendship grew and he confided in me on things he swore he never told another person. We shared those things that you might not want to admit to anyone else. I was privy to his pillow talk. I was his mistress before he even had a wife. Sadly, I did not know this was the case until fast forward 4 years later and I told him that I had met someone that I might really like. That guy turned out to be a joke and fodder for another tale, but he was the catalyst for a revelation. While Duncan and I were seeing each other, because I can't call it dating, for years and sharing secrets; he was dating someone else. At some point during those years, I recognized that he was not going to commit so I shared that I would not turn down other men who asked me out. Never did I give him up of course because I loved him, we were friends, and all the other lies I told myself to justify a travesty of a relationship that was going nowhere. Anyway, I wonder if I hadn't said anything how long it would have taken him to tell me. That is an answer I will never know. Well, he shared that he too had been seeing someone and it was progressing. She lived out of town but was actually planning to move to be with him. Instant heartbreak was mine. I mean I was totally and completely blindsided. I know it sounds stupid; but he was good, and I truly just wanted to be loved. He said the right things, and I convinced myself that I was the only person he was seeing because he was always around and seemingly always available. I see now how he managed to do that.

Let me tell you, I mourned that loss as if my pet had died. I straight up took to my bed and allowed the sadness to wash over me. Yes, I was dramatic but that shit hurt (sorry God for the cussing). How could he lie to me like this? He knew I was going to date other men, I told him that. He said nothing until a woman is moving into town, to live in his house, with him!!! It did not help that the guy I thought I might like turned out to be a total buster and unworthy of my time. I really need to make better choices but again, that's another tale for another time.

If I mourned the death of the relationship and moved on, how is it that I was now in bed with him? You see, I mourned him but like that famous third day resurrection and the hopes for the South after the Civil War, that thing rose again. Immediately after buster guy got kicked to the curb, I called him. As he has always done, he talked and listened and was my friend. Like I said, he was good. Besides, she wasn't here yet so what harm was there in still being around him? Y'all, I never said I was a scholar when it comes to love and relationships.

Two more years pass and I continue to date when I meet someone, he continues to be my friend and my lover and yes, the woman moved here to be with him. Well now I know how he had so much time. She was not around previously and once she got here she worked all the dang time. I mean I don't think she knew what an off day was. We had plenty of time to be together—early morning, afternoon, late nights. He came by after work, we met for "lunch" and the sex was awesome. We continued to share great conversations just about every day. We even had relationship issues without being a real couple. So many wrong things happened that I'm ashamed to share them. I had thoughts that she'd find out and be waiting for me. One day I'd leave the house that she shared with him and she'd be outside or would come in while we were in bed together. I swore the neighbors were going to tell her that, "hey, there's a woman who comes to your house whenever you aren't home." When I asked him about what if someone tells, he said "don't worry about it." He would often tell me not to worry because he had things under control.

Here's what I know, I did a great deal of wrong and I own it, but he did that and then some. He carried on with two women who loved and trusted him and genuinely thought she was the only one in his life at least until one of us found out the truth. But I digress, during the two years after she moved here, they decided to get married and planned a whole wedding. I mean a real legitimate, invitation, tuxedos, and nice venue wedding. I may be a little bit bitter at this so bear with me. He continued to call me and confide in me. We still regularly got together. He often told me that we were always going to be friends no matter what and he loved me. How do you love me when you are marrying someone else? Good question, too bad I didn't ask myself that enough. Around the time of the wedding, I just knew that I was going to walk away now because this was official. She was no longer his girlfriend, she was going to be his wife. Well, guess what? That didn't stop him. He called to make plans to see me because…sex. If you've ever dealt with a married man they have the same situation: she doesn't understand him, they don't have sex or it's not enough, he's only with her for the children, blah blah blah. I mean, I watch television, I've seen this before but as every teenage girl says about the bad boy her parents don't want her to date, "I love him!" I was a fool and he used it. Now, he will never admit that he used it and his explanation will be far more persuasive and different from mine, but he was the one getting married not me.

My man married another woman on a Saturday and was in my bed on Sunday morning because he loved me and was going to miss me while he honeymooned with his new wife. It was going to be a whole week before we could see each other and have sex again. I mean, we had to do it right? She simply was not giving him what he needed and he had me for that. I listened to him, I cheered him on, I gave him honest opinions and told him when I thought he was wrong. I was there for him and he loved me for that. How do I know? He told me, repeatedly. He played to my emotions and the love we had for each other. Did I continue to see him? Yep, sure did; up to and through his first anniversary only taking a break to give another man a real chance and because Duncan had pissed me off over something silly. When that other relationship didn't work out—I tend to cut off men fairly quickly because I somehow compare them to Duncan and they come up lacking—I went right back. This time, however, we started dating for real. This married man who I had known and been seeing for 7 years started actively dating me once he got married. He actually stepped his game up with me once he had a wife. I guess in an effort to keep me he realized he had to do more. He bought me gifts, gave me money, we went on dates in random public places that we didn't go to when he was single, he called more, we saw each other even more than before at his home and hotels. We set up how I would be included if anything ever happened to him—one of his children would reach out. This thing was real, strong and serious. The thing that I always wanted with him was actually happening but there was still someone else attached to it. That someone else made it easy because she was not around enough for me to even worry about. I could pretend she didn't exist, to an extent.

Then, God. I think through all of that God just got tired of me being a fool and said you know what, you are not happy and this situation needs to change. Just like that, I made a decision that I had to step away. Over the years I had always voiced that I wanted my own—my own man to do all the things we were doing but one who belonged to me. Duncan even told me that he wanted me to be happy and he knew the day would come that I would leave him for good. He admitted that he was jealous of any other man I saw and that he knew it was wrong because of his situation but that was just how he felt. He wanted me happy but with him. He even suggested that once I found that man for me that we could still see each other. He would be okay with that.

Well I decided I was not okay with that and after eight years, I made a change that focused on me. I gave him a date that our relationship would morph into something different. I stopped sleeping with him, but he kept asking. I stopped talking to him for a period to get myself prepared for the break and he reached out through his son to tell me he loved me. After that set period, I felt that I could still possibly be his friend but in the literal sense of the word, one without benefits. He swore that without my friendship he would miss me and things would not be the same because he was used to being able to vent out his frustrations to his eager ear, me. He needed me to be there for him but to hell with what I needed. See, I was finally open to seeing things how they really were. He needed me, and it was all about him and his needs.

I have stuck to my guns on this and I am feeling good about it. He is still married; I am still not but I'm working on my karma and asking God to forgive me. I am however, dating someone that I am giving an honest chance to build something. He still calls me to ask if I am coming over. I still refuse. He is still married.

The End

Now some may be blushing and asking why I would include this type of story in this book. It is because this story had an impact on the next one. During my seven years of being single and satisfied, I was aware of women (not just this one) who were receiving more attention from married men than I was from anyone. I used to joke and tell people that I couldn't buy a date. I had no male attention, no dates, no one whose head I turned. And eventually towards the end of my dating hiatus I questioned my value and my worth.

There were times I felt hopeless as if meeting someone would never happen, and other times I was resentful. To know that there were women who were actively seeing married men and in "relationships" that looked like what I wanted made me envious and eventually open to meeting someone. Dare I say anyone? Yes, sometimes it gets to that point for single people. Lord, does anyone want me? And so the timeline of the second season of my dating season begins.

Chapter 4

The Timeline

If you are reading this book for the gory details of the second disastrous relationship, I hate to disappoint you. Those details won't be in this book. It's too fresh and too raw. However, this story has three main characters: me, him, and God. One of the reasons he is not the main character is because in this relationship it was never about him. He told me from the very beginning where I stood. I was one of many so I stood at the bottom. It was clear in the disconnection, the lack of time, the callous treatment, and eventually his level of comfort of telling me about the other women.

But for me, because I was starving for attention and affection, I was willing to take whatever he gave. I walked away about a year and a half in for the very reason I ended up walking away at the end. Again, because of being starved for attention and affection, I came back when he said he missed me.

My best friend asked me to look at the pattern. She said he knows what to do to get you back. He knew to do just enough to reel me back in, and I went back like a moth to a flame. Where was God in all of this?

I walked away the first time because of the other women. Initially he wasn't so "in my face" with it, but it got worse over time. I thought I had made a clean break. I prayed and asked God to heal my heart. At this point in the fiasco, I had to pray every night just to be able to sleep at night. This was right as I was finishing my first book…maybe 15 pages left to write. I had to schedule my author's photo shoot with tears in my eyes. I had to use extra makeup to make sure my eyes wouldn't appear red in the photos for the book. Over time I dated someone else (another poor choice), but eventually I went back.

Normally I would be able to tell you what God was saying at that time, but I can't. I already know that I had turned down the voice of God as well as the direction of His Spirit. I walked not blindly but with eyes wide open back to the same person who hurt me from the beginning.

And here is where God came in. I would see him, and God would give me terrible dreams about who he was as a person. In the most disturbing of dreams, he had snakes coming out of his face, and I woke up with a start. I'm laughing as I tell you that I had the nerve to ask God what He was trying to say. No, not funny at all. I knew what God was saying and what He was showing me, but I stayed anyway.

A few months after going back to him we had a women's conference at my church, and Priscilla Shirer was the guest speaker on the first night. That night she prayed powerfully that every relationship that was not of God would be broken away from us. I lifted my hands, cried, and said yes, Lord. And I stayed with him. Well, not really stayed because remember, I was nothing to him. I was one of many, so what I did was wait to be called and I answered and kept entertaining the idea of the fake relationship I created in my mind. I had an incredible amount of shame. God had sent a powerful word through this woman, yet I was still ignoring the message that screamed, GET OUT!

I remember praying years ago that God would reveal things to me that were hidden in order to protect my heart. God did His part and revealed much to me, but I didn't respond. I am so ashamed of how much I wanted this person's attention and how much I wanted to be chosen.

Another New Year's Eve came and went. I can recall at least twice that the Spirt of God spoke into my spirit…Don't take him with you into the New Year. He cannot go where I'm taking you. Well, I had heard God whisper that before when I had yet to finish writing my first book. I could see areas in my life that God was blessing even though I was unequally yoked so I continued to drag my feet and delay leaving this horrible mess I was in. Thank God for His favor, but I was telling myself a dangerous lie. I could rationalize that my disobedience hadn't caused God to stop showing me favor nor had he closed any doors for me. This person himself made a statement that the world is the way it is today because God doesn't strike us down like He did in the Old Testament times. Clearly he was speaking from experience, and I could agree because I too had not been struck down. I knew the stories of people in the Old Testament who were disobedient, and God would wipe them out immediately. And there I was skating by, caught up with someone who had the potential to kill my spirit and soul, and disregarding the strong messages God was giving me to break away.

When I tell you there were red flags, billboards, and his own words that said: I'm treating you like crap, yet here you are accepting the crumbs that I'm throwing at you. I don't like using the word pathetic, but that's exactly how I felt. I was digging myself into a pit of self-loathing and self-disgust but still smiling around a person who was killing me internally.

Another year of foolishness from my side, and then God sent an even stronger message through my pastor. It was in the month of November, and I was driving to a Zumba event. Because it was a Sunday and I was missing church, I drove listening to my pastor online. Just like before I can't tell you what the message was, but I wept and wept; and the weeping was like a cleansing. All I can tell you was that the message was about the Holy Spirit and how this was going to be a season where the Holy Spirit was going to take TOTAL control over our lives if we allowed Him to. I was in my car crying, Yes, Lord! Yes, Lord! I will not go back (notice at that point I wasn't using the word never). I will not go back to him. I will not go back to sin and disobedience. I am saying yes to You, and I will be sold out for only You.

Brace yourself. It gets ugly from here.

I broke away for about three months. I was prepping to write two more books and to start writing my blog. I was in contact with him, but I kept saying I couldn't see him. Unfortunately, slowly I got caught back up, and God wasn't pounding me or speaking loudly at least for a little while. Instead one night I had a dream that was completely unreal, and I knew it was God shaking me with His own frustration and for my conviction.

In the dream this person was everything I always wanted him to be. We were having a conversation, and he was asking me about church. He was telling me that he wanted to go to church with me and that he was ready for more. I'm ashamed to say that I woke up and said, God, why would You show me something that will never happen? God didn't answer. He didn't have to. He had confronted me yet again with my stubbornness and why my stubbornness was going to lead to my own destruction.

I said yet again I can't do this and tried to walk away. God specifically and clearly told me to break off ALL communication. ALL! Guess what I told God? I told God that it would be mean to cut off all communication and that I could handle talking to him without actually going back. And then God let it happen.

God allowed me to SEE exactly why I could not go back. This person sent me a text and a picture that is too shameful to speak of, and my heart was shattered. My face was hot with shame. My heart was obliterated.

Now here's the part that is still murky to me in terms of what God was saying or doing. I know clearly that the path I took in those three years was not His will for me. He made it crystal clear that I was heading toward destruction. But in His grace and His allowance of our free will, He let me go foolishly into the abyss. I do believe even in that God left me with two options in the end, and what I experienced was the result of the path (the option) I chose. In my heart of hearts I know that God needed me to see the lowdown, dirty shame to let me know that I HAD to walk away this time. On the other hand, I believe He tried to protect me weeks earlier when He instructed me to cut off all communication. I don't know because this is a hard one. With one picture, God sealed the deal that there would be no return. The deeper part is with one picture, I vacillated between sharing my pain with others or burying it where no one would find it. I'm leaning toward God wanting me to see what I saw so that I would go through three things: first, the picture and text were my very own crucifixion and death of something God never wanted for me in the first place. In that one moment, I was hurt to the point that it could have been beyond repair. But God! Second, I was buried. I spent the next day wrestling with tears and with faith. The tears because it was finally over, and I had gotten nothing meaningful out of it. The faith because I had made God a promise after the other soul-crushing relationship. I promised God that I would never again get that lost in a losing relationship and wind up crying hopelessly over a man. In addition, I promised Him that I would never again lose my relationship with Him in the pursuit of a relationship with a man. So I cried for a few moments, wiped my tears, and said to myself no more tears. Last but certainly not least, all of this led to the resurrection of the Angie God ordained from the beginning of time.

I was called by God to write twelve years ago. The initial calling was to write daily devotionals, but clearly God had more for me to write. I heard a message recently that God doesn't show you everything from the beginning because you just might not accept the assignment. In addition a friend of mine told me years ago that God was going to use all of my life for His glory and that there would be no hiding certain chapters from my overall story. This is definitely one chapter I wish had never happened. I became a person I hated and who lived in shame and sadness because of what I was allowing in my life. No one forced me to be here, but this was a place I chose to be, which became a painful decision to live with.

On one hand I feel like I had a season of forfeiting the plan of God. I don't know. I was still blogging and writing for my fitness page, but I wasn't writing the books with substance that He called me to write. Not only that, I was living a secret life. I was drawn to darkness when He was calling me to not only be in the light but to be a light. Thank God for the many chances He gives us, and this tale is definitely one of the grace and mercy of God.

I was thinking one Sunday about this sad episode in my life and talking to God about the shame and embarrassment. There was a part of me that did not want any of THIS to appear on paper, but God gave me a message to give to some of you. This is the kind of God He is. He is the kind of God who can take a mess of a life, clean it up, and use it as a message to others for His glory. He is a forgiving and loving God. He can take broken people, pour out His Spirit, and build them back up stronger than before.

What do we do with all of the brokenness we encounter in this life? We give it back to God and allow Him to use it for His glory. At this season in my life I have seen people do one of two things after traumatic experiences. Some people stay down and never get back up, while others who once had faith lose their faith in the aftermath. I know of many who have fallen away by walking away from church and from God. Early in my Christian faith I knew I was supposed to point people to the love of Christ, but I never imagined it would be like this. To God be all the glory for having a plan for me even when I could not see it. To God be all the glory for having a plan to use even the worst parts of my life to bring glory to Him.

Chapter 5

How Did I Get Here A Second Time?

I got here because of the poor choices I made. I can say that I was influenced by friends, but the reality is I wrestled with the two women within me. I wrestled with the church girl who wanted to be in the forefront and the lonely woman who was hiding how much she wanted love and attention.

At some point I want to write a book called "Church Girl." It would not be the typical biopic of a stereotypical church girl: strict upbringing and knowing the Lord at an early age and never straying. No, this church girl, this writer, didn't have that experience…at least not fully. There is a wild streak in this church girl, and that is why it is often hard for me to imagine God doing two things: loving me unconditionally and being able to use me in His kingdom. I know that the word says that He loves me, and I often feel that love. But let me explain my struggle cognitively.

There are two men in the Bible who had name changes. Paul was first named Saul, and Israel used to be named Jacob. Before his name changed to Paul, Saul persecuted Christians. He was so feared by Christians that some of them were skeptical of Paul's conversion. Jacob's name meant trickster until God changed his name to Israel, which meant prince. Jacob was the grandson of Abraham and was destined for greatness, but his habit of conning people led him to have troubled relationships with his family and in his business dealings. Now ultimately both Paul and Israel were used powerfully by God in spite of how they started. In terms of relating to these stories of conversion, I recognize areas in my own life that God has changed and areas that He is still changing within me. Studying these two helped me to realize that most of us have two people within us. There is the person who wants to live for God and follow His leading, but there is another person within us who wants to live for ourselves and who wants to do what we want to do even if we are choosing to do what is sinful and wrong.

What did God see in Paul and Israel, and what does He see in us? I'm no Bible scholar on this one, but my heart is telling me that God saw their tenacity. Saul before he was Paul took a strict approach to how Jewish law should be followed, and he saw the early Christians as being blasphemous for following this new religion called Christianity. To Saul it was only right to stand up for his beliefs by executing the people who were breaking God's laws. That is until Jesus appeared before him on the road to Damascus. The newly named Paul would never be the same, and the New Testament couldn't have been fully written without him. Israel came from great stock, Abraham and Isaac. He was one of the patriarchs and would be the father of Judah, who was in the lineage of Jesus. But wasn't he a conman? Didn't he trick and scheme to get what he wanted? Yes, but in a pivotal moment when Jacob was all alone he wrestled with what some say was an angel or a man of God. While wrestling, Jacob said that he would not let go until the angel or man blessed him. That is tenacity. I believe that God is looking for faithful and tenacious people. People who are strong in their beliefs and have the gumption to strongly follow those beliefs. What happens along the way is that many of us are faithful in how we pursue what we want, whether it's right or wrong, and that shows our tenacity. We are strong and refuse to be quitters. But for many of us, we have to be redirected in order to follow the right pursuits with the type of passion and tenacity that God is looking for. When we submit our will to God, then He channels that passion and uses it for His kingdom and for His glory.

I did grow up with strict parents, and I did grow up in church. However, as a child my mom put me in dance classes, and I learned to love music and shaking my posterior at an early age. So for a long time there has been an internal struggle between the church girl and the dancer. I won't tell you how many solo dance recitals I performed in our basement. Needless to say, I have probably been dancing forever. As I got older I realized that I liked inappropriate music. You know the kind you turn down or off when your parents walk into the room. That was me. I still loved Jesus and praise music, but let something raunchy come on, and I forgot I was saved. What does this have to do with broken relationships? It has to do with the two people within us who sometimes duke it out: the holy and the profane. It has something to do with our thoughts and how what we listen to affects our thoughts.

I recognize within myself the wild streak and the one who wants to do what SHE wants to do. In fact at the beginning of the year I thought of this hashtag that says #IloveJesusandtrapmusic. When I sing sacred music, I think of the divine. When I listen to raunchy or trap music, my mind wanders to dark places where it shouldn't be. Don't all of our minds wander? The question is how often do we go to the places our minds wander? So there it is, as a woman I can admit my mind isn't always on holy things, but don't we usually assign this judgment to something that only men do? We think that men are always thinking sexually or inappropriately when all of us have indulged in mentally going down the wrong path and then sometimes acting on those thoughts.

In my fitness life, I would say that the body goes where the mind tells it to go. If I hate working out in the mornings, the only way my body will perform at zero dark hundred is to make up in my mind to get up and go. The only way my body will either give into or resist temptation is if my mind makes the decision to stray or stay faithful. I am not saying to never listen to secular or raunchy music. That's a grown folks decision. The point is there is a constant wrestling match within all of us to do what's right or to go astray. Likewise, many of us know that the people we have chosen to connect ourselves with are not good for us, but that wild streak within us says we can handle it and not get burned. Unfortunately many of us have the second and third degree burns as evidence that that simply isn't always true.

Chapter 6

The Questions

In addition to my faith, I have been blessed with a strong support system. As I shared with my closest friends what happened this time around, they asked me some questions that I think will help many of us as we navigate our relationships.

The first question a friend asked me was, "What kind of place were you in emotionally to allow this to happen?" She wasn't being critical at all. She was getting me to be self-reflective. My first response was a grimace on my face, but she certainly gave me some things to think about. I know I felt unloved and unlovable. Being single for so long without any prospects eventually got in my head. I saw singleness as rejection so I eventually got to the place where I would accept minimal commitment just so that I could say someone was at least kind of interested in me, and that's just skimming the surface. I truly was a person I thought I would never be.

Many of us replay the negative words that have been spoken over us, but there are also negative voices within our own minds. In my singleness I have had to consciously work on saying what God would say rather than what I conjure up on my own. For example, when I look at how long I've been divorced, I do wonder if I will ever find one person for me. Because I have so many friends who are over 40 and single, I can look at the situation as being dire. With those thoughts come the negativity. Can I tell you what doesn't help? It doesn't help when married people say, "He's coming," to which I have been known to say, "But I've been to the funerals of single women." Yeah, many people don't like when I say that, but it's true. Maybe people think they are being helpful when they say it and envision themselves giving single people hope, but can we also be realistic? I thought about including the stats on divorce, marriage, and singleness but decided against it. Most of us don't care about big statistics. We care about what is in our own world and sphere of influence.

In my sphere I have a tribe of professional, educated women. These women are established in their careers and may or may not have children. Some of my friends who are single and have never been married or had children wonder if it will happen. My friends and I who are divorced with children wonder if we will find a second partner and have the relationship we did not have in our twenties. Those are our realities. So when my friend asked what kind of emotional state I was in, I can honestly say I was not in a good place emotionally.

The next question was, "Would you allow your women friends to treat you the way he treated you?" This is the question I wish she had asked me in the beginning, and in all honesty, she probably did. These two questions came from a very good friend who has walked me through and talked me through everything. I remember calling her other times crying, and she calmly listened and asked me self-reflective questions. But I don't remember this one because the answer is a hands-down easy question to answer. I write and coach about women empowerment all the time, and I always tell women to "go where you're celebrated not tolerated." Wouldn't you know I did not take my own advice? Thankfully all of the women in my life have the gift of encouragement, and I am blessed to be able to spend time with people who uplift me and people whom I can uplift. I try very hard not to do petty or backbiting, nor do I believe in treating others in ways I don't want to be treated. Yet there I was in this place for three years with someone who could care less about me. A side note on the story in the middle: When I was envious of my friend who was being showered with time and attention from the married man, I only saw one side of the equation. She was getting attention, and I was not. Looking back now, my friend said it perfectly. The relationship was about what was convenient and beneficial for him, and she was an afterthought. I was in the same situation but realized it too late.

The final question came from another friend. With one question, she set my shattered heart and mind at ease. "Was this God's best for you?" Do I even need to answer this question? Of course he was not—not at the beginning and definitely not at the end. How had I veered so far off course of what God planned for me? It didn't happen overnight. It was convincing myself that spending time with someone was okay in the beginning until my feelings got involved but were not reciprocated. Slowly over time I was hooked and lying to myself that it wasn't as bad as I thought. It was much worse. The conversations and the actions of both men are clear indications that this was not God's best for me.

I pray that people reading this book will go into future relationships asking yourselves these questions and answering them honestly. I spent a lot of time either in denial or disappointed in myself for being in this place. One thing that my friend did ask me to do is to start keeping a personal journal. I blog and share all of the time, but I do believe I need a space that is just for me. Maybe keeping a relationship journal or any kind of journal that is just for you will help you be honest with yourself. In addition I encourage you to get an accountability partner. Raising my hand on this one, we can do a lot of foolish things on our own free will. If it seems like a good idea to us, we go all in. I certainly have done it. When I talk to my rational friends, they often won't even have to say anything. They just look at me with the stare that says, "Are you crazy?", to which I usually laugh and say out loud what I was conjuring up in my own mind. Just like accountability works in fitness, it also works in helping us make better decisions.

I Have Questions

Just like my friends had questions for me, I had questions for God. I knew how I had gotten to this place. I had chosen the wrong man with full knowledge of who he was and what he was about. My question for God began with why it felt so much like a spiritual attack. Because maybe it was.

I took a long walk on the beach, but this time without any headphones, music, or any distractions. Just the sound of the waves and birds. There I was left alone with my thoughts and then my questions. God, what is all of this about? My first thought was all the way back to the beginning with Eve. Notice that the devil didn't appear to Adam first. He first appeared to Eve, which got me wondering why. What was so powerful about Eve that the devil set a trap for her? The longer I thought about the devil, the longer I thought about his plan for her. The devil wanted to deceive Eve by making her feel that what God had for her wasn't enough. It wasn't enough that God created this whole garden for you, Eve, and gave you everything you could ever need or want in that garden. There was something in you that said it still isn't enough. I began to think about myself. For years I thought I had enough. I had the career I wanted, the material possessions, the family, and friends. But something was missing. At first I thought I wanted companionship, but it turned out I was looking for one thing. Validation. I wanted someone to affirm me and make me feel that I was important. That I mattered. I was willing to be deceived by the person in front of me even though I knew he cared nothing about me. I pretended that he cared about my thoughts, but I couldn't pretend that he cared about my feelings because it was clear that he didn't. Which leads me back to the first question I had for God…why did this feel like a spiritual attack? Because it was.

Going back to the beginning of my own calling, God first required one thing of me and that was to write. Jesus said that out of the abundance of the heart the mouth speaks. (Or in this case out of the abundance of my heart I would write.) Whose heart could have abundance when it's broken? Not mine…at least it wasn't overflowing with abundance. Whose mind could be focused when I was wondering if this man was ever going to see me the way I wanted him to see me? Certainly not my mind. I remember time and time again I would tell him I couldn't do this thing with him because I needed to focus on my writing. We wouldn't communicate for awhile, but he would always draw me back in and tempt me with the attention and validation I desperately wanted. Looking back now that it is over, I see my role in it as well as the hand of the enemy and his master plan. The enemy wanted to stop what God had for me by getting me to think just like Eve. God, I know you have given me much, but it still isn't enough. As a result of searching for and finding the wrong thing, had I been hurt beyond repair I would have forfeited my calling.

Chapter 7

The Parallels

When you make two terrible decisions, you have to take a step back and ask yourself, what was I thinking? Even though all that time had passed between the two people, I still had to examine how I was in a bad situation twice and why had I not learned the lesson the first time. The first parallel I made between these two relationships had to do with the length of time I was involved. I remember looking at the second person and saying, "I don't stay anywhere past one year, especially if I know it's not going anywhere." Yep. Those were my words. He never made me any promises, and in fact said he wasn't trying to be committed to anyone. After I said it at the end of year one, I remember now how smug I felt thinking I was still in control of my emotions. Clearly I wasn't. Reflecting on how drastically I was affected by someone else's addiction in the first relationship, I should have learned that emotions can take you down a dangerous road of codependency. How often do we convince ourselves that we can't live without someone even though they are detrimental to us emotionally and that we know that there is no good future for us if we stay?

The other parallels include my relationship with God at the time and my relationships with my friends. In both relationships, I thought I was still walking with God, but let's look deeper. In the first relationship over time I became incredibly angry with God. I was angry because God was not fixing his drinking problem. At the time I had a close friend who told me if I would pray hard enough and fast long enough God was going to turn things around. Please run from people who tell you things like this in this type of circumstance. This man had been an alcoholic for years, and this was NOT the relationship God had for me. Yet in my mind I believed that my salvation and faith would set him free. It is one thing to have friends that encourage you to stay strong in bad situations, but this was not only bad. This is not where I was supposed to be. It now saddens me that I allowed someone else to convince me that I had the power to change an alcoholic. No one has that power except them and God.

In the second relationship I wasn't angry with God. I was angry with myself. I knew from the first day that I wasn't supposed to be involved with him, but I chose poorly and stuck with my poor decision. The first year was more so fun and games, and then things went south. I was angry, hurt, and jealous—often feeling inadequate and questioning what was wrong with me. Not once did I look at God and blame Him for this mess because this mess had only one name on it—mine.

The last parallel has to do with shame and embarrassment. One night my friends and I attended an event on a cold winter night, and we had to park far from our venue. As we were walking towards the parking lot, they spotted a familiar van in the parking lot of a bar and asked if we could go in and get a ride from Adam. I was mortified because I knew what we would find once we walked inside. Sure enough he was already drunk trying to play it off, and my face was red with heat and shame. To be with him was constant embarrassment about his actions. I knew he was never an angry drunk, but he definitely wasn't able to handle his liquor well which made his behavior unpredictable. It's one thing when you are alone with an alcoholic, but it's different when you are amongst friends. Very few friends knew the extent of Adam's drinking or how sad I was, so this was yet another time I was trying to downplay the severity of the situation. He ended up driving us to our cars, but I was torn up inside.

As far as the other person is concerned, I had a different type of embarrassment and shame. No one ever saw us together so only I knew the ugliness that was who we were together. I always told myself I wouldn't accept being last to other women, but I had accepted it. I don't know yet how to get over that. I don't know how to feel like I'm enough when I wasn't. That is still a part of my healing process. All I know is it is a hard place to be when you become the person you thought you would never be: openly rejected and accepting of being rejected.

Chapter 8

The Aftermath

God began my healing process by reminding me of what He called me to do and reminded me of when I was first called to write. I love this story! It was during the interlude of this journey, and I was at a Life Empowerment conference at a church in Richmond. I was sitting in a session on fasting, and I distinctly heard God call me to write. Now it had been a long time since I had received instructions from God, at least instructions that were that specific. The Spirit had spoken words of comfort and direction to me, but this was so detailed that I was amazed. I was already in the midst of an intense Bible study and was close to finishing the whole Bible at that point. The Spirit spoke to me to write down what He said and to put it into a daily devotional. My first response was, Lord, nobody wants to hear what I have to say. He said it would be Him speaking through me.

I lay that down for a long time, only halfheartedly writing some things down in a notebook, but it would be years before I recognized that I was doing what God called me to do.

At this point I've been writing for five years. First there was a fitness page, a book, and then a daily blog. Guess how the fitness page came to be? God had told me months before to create a fitness page on Facebook, but again I responded with the mantra that nobody wants to hear what I have to say. That seems to be a recurring theme, which is interesting since I truly do love to write and to share. Our own self-doubt will often forfeit what God has for us and not outside forces. When problems arise, it's not the problems that stop us. It is what we tell ourselves about the problem. When this disaster happened, the last thing I wanted to do was to tell people what happened. I certainly didn't want to put this awful chapter on paper that would be read by people I thought might judge me and my poor decisions. But this is why I had to get past those thoughts and feelings.

As I was sharing with other women about the topic of the book, it inspired many to tell me their own stories. I remember sitting with one friend over lunch and vowing I wasn't going to share anything. Of course I shared. And then she shared. Then we talked about including her story in this book. I believe when she made that decision it gave her power back to her. Sometimes we get lost in relationships, especially the dysfunctional ones. We spend so much time trying to fix the dysfunctional relationship that we are doing no other good for ourselves or for the people in our community who need us. Other times, we go through life existing but not really living.

Here's something else that women shared with me. A few women told me that they were surprised that I was writing about two relationships. Many of them told me that after the first heartbreak they stopped opening themselves up to a chance for love. I completely understand. I can see how being burned once means that you make the decision to live single and to refuse to risk getting hurt again. But here's another look at what it means to live a life with no risks. During the interlude when I was serving God and being a workaholic, I wasn't doing anything dynamic for God. I was serving safely in my church as a greeter and a Sunday school teacher. I didn't reach anyone outside of the church walls. It turns out that just like Jesus needed Judas to get to the cross, I needed my own Judas to get me to the place where I could write THIS book. I had other "safe" books in my mind, but this is the one that needed to be written and read. I've learned both as a reader and a writer that our stories can help someone else get free and begin to live again.

Years ago I read "Eat, Pray, Love" by Elizabeth Gilbert, and the one part of the story that gripped by heart is when she writes about being so unhappy in her marriage that she was curled up in a ball on the cold bathroom floor feeling total despair. When I read that book, I felt her pain. I had lived her pain. It helped me to read her journey back to self-love and wholeness. Did she hurt like hell before she got to that place? Absolutely! Did she recover? Absolutely! In this aftermath, I learned that there is a purpose to our pain. It isn't just for us, but it is also for the people who will come behind us and who need to know that survival is possible.

Once I started my weight loss journey and going to dance fitness classes, I met all kinds of people. As we got to know each other we started sharing pieces of our lives and pieces of our hearts. I've met women in unhappy situations whom I never would have known were in those situations based on their energy and their smiles in class. That is one of the reasons I wanted to write this book. When heartache and heartbreak come, we have two choices. We can stay down and check out of living a real life, or we can take the bull by the horns and keep moving while we are healing. This book was a part of my healing, but be assured I never stopped moving. My mom taught me to never let the devil steal my joy, and I have to work to do what she told me. I have tried my best on this journey to both laugh and dance. When things get really bad, I call my friends who make me laugh. I go to my classes where my fitness sisters always make me laugh and we enjoy dancing together. For my mom and my sisters, I have kept myself moving.

Chapter 9

Relationships and Spiritual Warfare

Have you recognized within yourself the moment that you saw God growing you up and maturing you? I'm famous for crying, me, me, me, and wondering why God is silent, and then God allows more life to happen to me in order for me to see the bigger picture of what He was doing all along. I have a tendency to see myself first and the big picture second, but God opened my eyes to see so much more than what I was seeing. For a long time, longer than I care to admit, I saw having a relationship as something to fulfill my selfish needs. I wanted time and attention, and I thought that because I wasn't asking for material goods that I was being super spiritual and deep. I thought I just wanted time and companionship, but now that I reflect on it more what I actually wanted was for someone to think highly of me and spend time with me and cater to me. Boy that's a lot of "mes", and that is how I missed the boat on this one.

"How could one chase a thousand, and two put ten thousand to flight, unless their Rock had sold them, and the Lord had surrendered them?" (Deuteronomy 32:30)

I was studying the book of Job for another book I'm writing, and I kept coming back to the fact that in the first chapter Satan approached God before he does anything to Job. Job was a blameless and upright man, and Satan asked for permission to take everything away from Job because he thought Job would curse God. Job lost everything and didn't curse God. In another set of calamities Job lost his health and was covered in boils. Again, Job did not curse God. What does this have to do with relationships? In all that Job lost, he did not lose his wife. This isn't in the Bible, but I can imagine that maybe he wished he had based on her response to Job's condition. Job 2:9-10 states, "This his wife said to him, 'Do you still hold fast to your integrity? Curse God and die!' But he said to her, 'You speak as one of the foolish women speaks. Shall we indeed accept good from God, and shall we not accept adversity?' In all this Job did not sin with his lips."

Now wait a minute? The book of Job starts out describing him as an upright man. Does an upright man curse God? He might if he is attached to the wrong person. In the worst chapter of Job's life, his so-called friends came to see him and did everything except speak life into his situation. Then he had the added pressure of listening to his wife, his life partner, also speak more death into what he was going through. It was during this time of studying that I saw the bigger picture of relationships.

Every day we wake up we have spiritual forces operating all around us. Oftentimes we ignore it or some of us don't believe those forces are real, but I see these forces at work more and more the older and more aware I become. For example, sickness and disease can be a form of spiritual forces at work. Most of us can agree that sickness does not come from God, but He allows it to impact some of us at various stages of our lives. I have friends who have children who were born with chronic health issues. These parents are faithful believers, and they have prayed for their children's healing and health. However, I have seen some of these children go in and out of the hospital yet continue to succeed in academics, in sports, in friendships, and in life in general. These children with chronic health problems, as well as their parents, had choices in terms of how they would react to the crisis. They could trust God and move forward, or they could get angry and curse God. What do you do when you have two parents on opposite sides? It makes it much harder to fight the good fight of faith.

This is an extreme example, but doesn't life hit us in extreme ways? Over the years that I dated these two men who were wrong for me, there were times I know that I was dealing with a fight with a spiritual force behind it. I had issues at my job, issues with my health (chronic back pain), issues with my finances, and issues with my son. In none of these cases could I go to the man I thought I was connected with and pray. None. That sounds so sad now looking back that I did not see the importance of just having a partner I could pray with. I was so busy focusing on having someone that I didn't look at the purpose of being in a real God-ordained relationship and that is to do the will of God and to bring glory and honor to God. It's hard to bring glory and honor to God when one partner has a strong faith life and wants to do the will of God and the other is worldly and wants little or nothing to do with God.

I grew up hearing the scriptures about not being unequally yoked, but I did not understand the impact until I was unequally yoked. Being with someone who is Bible believing, faithful to God, and sees prayer as a priority brings an added blessing to the relationship. On the worst days a prayerful partner can bring light and life to your situation.

Maybe you are reading this and wondering how I could be so lost and so blind. I will answer that for myself and surmise how someone else might have been lost and blind. I was lost because I saw myself and what I wanted more than I saw God's will for my life. I saw that I had been by myself for a long time and because these men were not horrible people (at least not in the beginning), I thought I could be attached to an unbeliever and come out unscathed. I was wrong. My spiritual life was affected by being unequally yoked, but thank God for His grace.

Do you remember the oddly placed story of Tamar in the midst of the telling of Joseph's story? Well, both the stories of Tamar and Joseph are stories of redemption. No matter how far we go on our own free will God is still waiting for us to follow the steps He has already ordered. No matter what has been done to us beyond our control like Joseph God still has a plan to work everything out.

Being in wrong relationships can very much be like spiritual warfare. Depending on the dynamics of wrong relationships, how you interact with someone who wasn't sent by God can damage your faith a little or completely destroy it. I pray that you believe in the redemptive love of God and know that ultimately you can get back into His perfect will. His perfect will is for us to be in the right relationships where we work together to use our gifts and walk out our callings. In His perfect will, we join with others to fight spiritual battles together with the power God has given us. But what if you feel like you have gone too far from His will? You ask for forgiveness, believe that you have received His forgiveness, and get back into His will. In His permissive will, God will wait for us to return and to walk out the path He had all along, but it is never too late to return to Him.

As I learned in the previous broken relationship, I knew I had to turn to the word of God for healing. The beauty was because I had studied the word for so long, I didn't even have to open up my Bible or Bible App. The word was down deep inside me. Whether I was in motion or still, verses I have known for years came to mind and gave me peace. As I close this portion of the book, I pray that these scriptures will give you peace, hope, and courage. What looked like it would take you out was only the stepping stone that gave you a greater purpose. Be encouraged because this is only the beginning of the great things God has in store for you. I look forward to hearing your testimony of healing and restoration.

Chapter 10

Words of Healing and Restoration

Day 1

"He makes me to lie down in green pastures; He leads me beside the still waters. He restores my soul…" (Psalm 23:2-3)

The 23rd Psalm was the first passage of scripture I had to memorize as a Sunday school student back when I was terrified to speak in public. I remember my great uncle was a deacon at the church, and he stood over me strongly urging me to open my mouth and say it loud. Deep sigh… It's not a matter of how loud you can say a verse. It's how well you know it in your heart. In the middle of the night this passage came to mind giving me peace. Some forty years later I understand what God is saying. I lead a busy life, and if I had it my way I wouldn't take any days off in terms of working out or writing. My schedule seems to be work, working out, writing, repeat; and it's one I've had for a long time. But as God is healing my heart and my mind, He is leading me to lie still so that my soul can be restored. There are times when we hurt so deeply that we might think that God isn't concerned. That isn't true. God is always concerned about us. In our busyness we may forget to settle ourselves and just be. Busyness may be a momentary distraction, but this is the time to rest your mind and your spirit and allow Him to heal your soul.

Day 2

"Yet in all these things we are more than conquerors through Him who loved us." (Romans 8:37)

This is not the end. Not only is it not the end, we cannot even conceive what God has for us next. It is the trick of the enemy to make us feel hopeless when we fall and to try to get us to stay down, but the devil is a liar. God said that we are more than conquerors. Do you know what God has said about you? Do you spend time rehearsing what God says or what other people have said about you? Better yet, what have you been saying about yourself? Ironically as I struggled with singleness and feeling unloved, I said several things about myself indicating just how low I had allowed my self-esteem to become. Constantly comparing myself to other women and always feeling less than. Am I not the same person who writes daily to encourage women to love themselves? Yet I was struggling because I felt I wasn't good enough to hold anyone's attention long enough to construct something that was real and lasting. Isn't it funny that in a world full of divorces, single people still want the chance to love and be loved? In addition, for many of us we attach our worth to whether or not we are in a relationship. Can you be a conqueror on your own? You sure can. I once was a conqueror—bold in my faith and my convictions. As I watched myself walk away from my convictions and to allow my self-worth to fade to black, my words and thoughts about myself suffered. But praise God for another chance to embrace what He has already said about us. I am more than a conqueror and so are you. You may have been defeated momentarily, but it is just that— momentary.

Day 3

Taking the First Step

"Being confident of this very thing, that He who has begun a good work in you will complete it until the day of Jesus Christ." (Philippians 1:6)

Maybe you're reading this and thinking, "That's nice, but I'm not there yet." Maybe the idea of facing what you went through is too painful and you don't see yourself getting over it, at least not right now. You don't have to. You can decide to take baby steps instead. The darkest days I ever faced were when my alcoholic boyfriend left me. I lay in my bed incredulously, not believing that it was over. Three years of loving someone and it was over. Three years of loving someone and he chose to throw the relationship and me away. It was a brutal blow to my self-esteem and ego as well as a stab in my heart. There was no bouncing back easily from that, but I knew I had to at least try to heal emotionally. I took baby steps every day to get healed. Honestly getting out of bed and going to work counted as a baby step. Functioning throughout the day was another small step. Avoiding crying in front of students and colleagues was a major step. And these were just the steps I took to get through the school day. Managing my emotional health at home was something else. I alternated at first between sadness and anger. How could someone choose alcohol over me? Wasn't I good enough? I had to do a lot of internal work to begin to feel adequate and good enough and to let the anger go. The strange part of the recovery was reaching the numb place—the place where I truly was just existing day to day, basically moving robotically through my daily life. By the time I got deeper into studying God's word and spending time in His presence I began to feel like myself again. Correction, I began to be better than I was before, and it all began with a tiny step forward.

Day 4

A Prayer of Restoration

It may seem strange that I'm going to include harsh language in a prayer devotional, but sometimes we have to face our harshest realities. There are times that my past makes me feel downright dirty. To quote a friend, "If you lie down with dogs, you get up with fleas." When she said it, I thought she was being cruel and insensitive, but I knew the moment she said it she was speaking truth. I had already been playing with fire thinking that I wasn't going to get burned. I moved deeper and deeper into the furnace, yet unlike the three Hebrew boys, there wasn't a fourth man in the furnace with me. It was just me and my bad decisions. And then I came out feeling dirty.

David wrote Psalm 51 after a time that I'm sure made him feel dirty. He had taken Bathsheba for himself and had her husband killed to cover up the pregnancy that followed their dalliance. He writes in verse 10, "Create in me a clean heart, O God, and renew a steadfast spirit within me." I encourage you to read the whole psalm because it is an example of what a repentant heart and mind sound like. I have prayed and asked God to forgive me for my part in these relationships. I have prayed and asked Him to keep my heart pure. This prayer isn't just for keeping a heart pure from sin and deceit but also from anger and bitterness. Typically the hardest part for me once the sadness is over is actually moving past the anger. I can replay in my mind repeatedly what I perceive as injustice and quickly lay blame on the offender. But as I've said often, I never was supposed to be in either of these relationships. Isn't it interesting how we can be upset and angry over the aftermath of a fiasco we played a part in? It's like getting angry after a car accident when you were speeding. I can see now that I might not have sped into wrong relationships, but I can acknowledge that I was speed walking straight into disasters. As a result, my heart was broken, and now comes the time for me to wait for my heart to be healed and purified again.

Day 5

It Was Never About You

"Therefore prepare yourself and arise, and speak to them all that I command you. Do not be dismayed before their faces, lest I dismay you before them." (Jeremiah 1:17)

Bless God, when I served in children's ministry my leaders told me that serving was never about me. On good days I could smile and agree. On rough days when I was in my feelings, I was frustrated and wondering how serving was benefitting me. Then I took a break from children's ministry and eventually started writing. In the early days I was sharing the successes and setbacks of getting fit and healthy. For the most part I never thought I was oversharing and was comfortable with telling my story. And then the shift came. I felt the drive to begin writing about my spiritual journey. Because of the bad relationship in the background there were times I felt guilty writing about God while being in turmoil emotionally and spiritually. Wrestling with myself and with what God was calling me to do. When everything crashed and burned, I had lunch with a friend. Before I could fill her in on the gory details, she was complimentary of my blog and everything I was writing. She looked at me and asked how I could write things that she was dealing with and we hadn't even talked. All I could do was hang my head and thank God for the gift. I was then reminded of what my children's ministry leaders had told me years ago. Serving is never about you. When I put words on paper, there is healing for me. But most importantly, there is a message that God has for people, and graciously and mercifully He allows me to write some of those messages. For those of you who are struggling with the calling on your life, especially on the roughest days, know that God has a plan not only for you but for every person who will receive the gift within you. The pain was never about you. It was to be a bridge for the next person and a sign to know that they will cross over and survive.

"Blessed by the God and Father of our Lord Jesus Christ, the Father of mercies and God of all comfort, who comforts us in all our tribulation, that we may be able to comfort those who are in any trouble, with the comfort with which we ourselves are comforted by God." (2 Corinthians 1:3-4)

Day 6

Trust Your Heavenly Father

"Trust in the Lord with all your heart, and lean not on your own understanding; in all your ways acknowledge Him, and He shall direct your paths." (Proverbs 3:5-6)

What makes these chapters of my life so difficult to write is that I had a wonderful earthly father. He was present, he was a provider, and he was supportive. Yet as an adult I chose the wrong path in relationships. I take the loss on that one. But I am more concerned about my sisters who grew up without a father. Maybe you are searching for the wrong man because you weren't raised by your father or any man, and there is a search for what you were missing. Maybe you didn't have a relationship with the Heavenly Father so there is a missing piece that makes you want to fill that missing piece with a man. As I write this completely unattached, I'm asking both you and me to trust our Heavenly Father to fill any voids we have in our lives. My personal struggle is with seemingly having everything except someone to share it with. I've been divorced almost 20 years, so I have taken the advice of pastors who say take yourself out to dinner and enjoy your singleness. But there are times I don't want to take myself out to dinner, yet on the other hand I don't want to go with just anyone and end up in the situations I was in before. A long, long time ago at the conference where I was first called to write, Juanita Bynum was a speaker at the conference, and she sang, "I Don't Mind Waiting." It's a beautiful song with an infectious melody, and the song became my Saturday morning worship song. I sang that song for years, but by the seventh year I guess I got tired of waiting and made my own path to find someone. You have read how that turned out. There is something funny that we say in church and that is when you've tried everything else and it failed, try God. It's funny yet sad; sad but true. I had no idea that I would be single this long, but I learned that not trusting God in this process led to unnecessary heartache and pain. As for me, it's time for me to trust the Father again.

Day 7

Keep Going

"The Lord is my light and my salvation; whom shall I fear? The Lord is the strength of my life; of whom shall I be afraid?" (Psalm 27:1)

It was a beautiful Wednesday night, and I was driving to Zumba like I do every Wednesday night. Class was wonderful, and the instructor's energy was beaming. I left class on a natural high, and with one text and picture my heart was crushed. Fast forward to a week later. I was actually smiling and excited, even though it was a rainier Wednesday night. As I was getting ready for class, I looked in the mirror and saw a genuine smile. I was glad to have something to hold onto as my heart healed. I have loved Zumba from the first time I took class with whom I affectionally call my Zumba mom. Over the years, I have met more instructors, but there is a spark in my Wednesday night instructor that sets my heart on fire every week. I'm sharing this story for my brokenhearted friends who have lost your spark. I know heartbreak hurts. If we aren't careful, a heartbreak (the initial act that broke your heart) will turn into heartache (a duller yet intense ache that seems like it will never end). My prayer for you is that you don't stay there. Get up, get moving, dance, sing, walk, stay active. Do something that will make both you and your heart smile again. I was so excited that second week knowing that I was going to dance rather than staying home and crying. Life has a way of knocking you down, and if you aren't aware, it will keep you down. Choose to get up and do something that is good for your health mentally, physically, and spiritually.

Day 8

"But you, beloved, building yourselves up on your most holy faith, praying in the Holy Spirit, keep yourselves in the love of God, looking for the mercy of our Lord Jesus Christ unto eternal life." (Jude 20-21)

In the spiritual realm the number eight is the number of new beginnings. Life happened, circumstances crumbled, yet here you are left standing. What are you going to do to rebuild your new self? Prayerfully you are going to already have faith to stand on, but if not, it's never too late to build your faith. What is faith? Faith is looking back over areas in your life that you have already conquered and recognizing that recovery is possible. The irony of me writing this second book is that my original plan was to have two other books completed before writing this. As I dealt with negative emotions over the past year I knew I couldn't produce the type of book God placed on my heart and not produce something that was unpolluted, especially a book on overcoming other adversities in my life. So how did

I get to the place that I could write this book? By faith. There is already one book by faith, so if God could work through me to produce one book, He can work in me to write several more. Do I want to even admit how many times my heart has been broken? The best answer is that my heart was only deeply broken once, and thankfully the pain of the other heartbreaks didn't last as long. The reason the other times didn't hurt as badly and as long is because I was already building my faith and praying in the Spirit. Everyone knows that hindsight is 20/20, yet that first heartbreak taught me to never again let anyone separate me from the love of Christ. As difficult as the last relationship was, I chose to hold onto God's hand even while I hung my head in shame. I trusted Him to love me and keep me even though I was out of His will. Just like the father waiting for the prodigal son, our Father has never lost sight of where we are and will still guide us back to where we need to be lovingly and with His never-ending mercy. Hold onto your faith and don't let go. A new and brighter day is coming for you.

Day 9

Today I prayed for you, and when I prayed I used the word tormented. I prayed for those of you reading this who are tormented by memories of a hurtful relationship. I prayed about the words that have been spoken to you that are hard to forget. I prayed for those who miss hearing someone tell you that they love you. I prayed for the condition of your heart and for the emptiness you feel. I have been there. I have gone out with friends with the intent to have a great time and not focus on that past relationship, but memories popped up and I had to fight back the tears. To me that is what it feels like to be tormented emotionally. My friend, this too shall pass. In Ecclesiastes 3:4 the word of God says that there is "A time to weep, and a time to laugh; a time to mourn, and a time to dance," and maybe today is your day to cry. But I implore you to acknowledge that there is an ending date to your crying.

I tend to be a happy person most of the time, especially when I'm teaching. Yet there were some days in the aftermath that my smile had faded. My mind was tormented with memories. A very sweet student glanced at me as I was working at my desk and asked, "Are you okay?" I answered honestly that I wasn't and then asked him how he knew. Such sensitivity from an 11 year old! Or was it a message from God saying that He too saw my fallen smile and was drawing me back into His presence where there is fullness of joy? On my worst days when I feel separated from God and my joy is depleted, I realize that it isn't God who has moved.

It is me. I have moved from the source of my joy, but He is waiting in the wings to receive me. If you find yourself feeling depleted, you don't have to stay on the outskirts of God's love. He's waiting right here for you.

Day 10

Reactions to Hurt

"Those who are planted in the house of the Lord shall flourish in the courts of our God. They shall still bear fruit in old age; they shall be fresh and flourishing, to declare that the Lord is upright; He is my rock, and there is no unrighteousness in Him." (Psalm 92:13-15)

As I was writing this book, I heard at least three preachers address the issue of church hurt. There are people who have chosen not to go to church because they have been hurt by someone or several people in a church they once attended. The preachers who addressed the issue made a valid point. How many of us have been hurt by someone at work? But we go to work anyway because work pays our bills and feeds our bellies. One preacher even said that sometimes the people within our homes hurt us, but we don't sleep outside. At the end of the day we go to our homes in spite of the ones who live with us who have hurt us. Why don't we have the same reaction to church? People call church a hospital for the sick, but the truth is all of life is a hospital for the sick. There are hurting and wounded people everywhere we go. The ones who don't wear masks are easy to identify, but all of us have some hurt within us. Where are you choosing to go to ease the pain? How are you dealing with the pain? In that first pivotal relationship I saw what it was like to mask pain with alcohol. I have also seen what it looks like to cut yourself off from everyone out of fear of being hurt again. When we cut ourselves off from everyone we miss out on the opportunity to be healed. A few years ago I lost an uncle to prostate cancer. As sad as his passing was, it was even sadder when I found out he had not been to see a doctor in 25 years. Twenty-five years!!! I can't imagine what types of ailments were missed and what kind of pain he endured over the years simply because he did not go for help. I know for some of my readers church is not for you. But for those who are open to trying church for the first time or maybe even a second time, I pray that you will consider going to hear a word that will help facilitate your healing.

Day 11

For Single Sisters Serving in Ministry

"Wait on the Lord; be of good courage, and He shall strengthen your heart; wait, I say, on the Lord!" (Psalm 27:14)

Girlfriend, I feel your pain. You know you are called to ministry, and you may even be serving in ministry. But you are single. If your singleness isn't an issue, you can stop reading here. However, for some of us, our singleness can feel like a curse somedays. I didn't say it is a curse. I said it can feel like a curse. For some of you, it may be your career and singleness that don't seem to mesh. You are successful and have attained every goal you have set for yourself. Yet you are still single. In fact it seems like you are going to be single forever. How do single sisters make peace with this? I don't have any easy answers. Some of the answers I have aren't going to sound kind to married people, but it's my perspective. In the nearly 20 years I have been divorced I know for sure that I don't want to be in an unhappy marriage. The times that I talk to God about finding someone I always add this: Lord, I don't want a husband. I want a companion. He has never answered me on that one, but He does send people who say the words I loathe hearing. "God doesn't want to give you a boyfriend. He wants to give you a husband." To which I either whine internally or aloud, "But I don't want a husband!" I know—it sounds jaded, but I'm not going to lie to you or myself. I know myself well enough to know I'm not ready for that level of self-sacrifice. Meanwhile there are others who do want to be married or at least in a committed relationship, but for whatever reason it hasn't happened yet. So we wait. What do we do while we wait? You've learned from this book that it's not the best idea to date just anybody while you wait—not at the risk of damaging your spirit and your soul. And God forbid we try to "help" God by looking on our own. So we wait. Prayerfully while we wait we allow God to strengthen us emotionally. Prayerfully we trust Him to fill the places that feel empty. I told you there were no easy answers, but I do know I would rather place my trust in God than to forge out my own path that might lead to my destruction.

Day 12

The Lifter of My Head

"But You, O Lord, are a shield for me, my glory and the One who lifts up my head." (Psalm 3:3)

It goes without saying that God's timing is the best. I knew I had at least three more books in me after writing the first book and started writing two of them last fall. After a season of turmoil, I knew that I had a story to tell about overcoming adversity. The problem was that one of those books was about losing material possessions, and my pride didn't want to put my truth on paper. But in the face of the poor decisions I made in that last relationship I learned that there is something worse than losing things. The worst thing I lost was myself. Pride? What pride? It's hard to have any pride left when you know that you are last to everything else in a man's life, especially a man you care about. I thought I had been kicked in the gut after being left for alcohol, but the last relationship? Nothing compares to that type of kick in the gut. But God! Because God was already working behind the scenes, He knew that there was yet another book in me—another story to tell. He knew that this book would be birthed out of chaos. He knew that He would settle my heart and mind to the point where I could put my truth on paper, stare it in the face, and release it to others.

I know there are no scriptures that say that Jesus Christ is like glue, but that is what His presence has been like for me. In the most broken times of my life, His Spirit was alive in me awakening every dead area and piecing back together every broken place. God wastes nothing. If you are alive and reading this, He still has a plan for your life. Scary as it may be and no matter how dark the hour, God can take that place and use it for His glory.

Day 13

Bounce Back. Don't Clap Back.

"Then Jews from Antioch and Iconium came there; and having persuaded the multitudes, they stoned Paul and dragged him out of the city, supposing him to be dead. However, when the disciples gathered around him, he rose up and went into the city. And the next day he departed with Barnabas to Derbe. And when they had preached the gospel to that city and made many disciples, they returned to Lystra, Iconium, and Antioch, strengthening the souls of the disciples, exhorting them to continue in the faith, and saying, 'We must through many tribulations enter the kingdom of God.'" (Acts 14:19-22)

Dear Injured Parties, as much as you want to, thou shalt not clap back. I know there may be something within you that wants to lash out and attack the person who injured you. For a season it may feel like it will be the thing that releases your own pain. I can assure you it won't. It isn't my nature to explode on people, but I have had friends who have advised me to do just that.

I was having a rough day emotionally, and I told my friend that I had just finished crying when she called. When I told her why I was crying, she asked me the following. "You didn't cuss him out?" I laughed and said no. No, I don't cuss people out. I get mad, and I might cuss to myself; but I will not give anyone the satisfaction of knowing that they took me out of character. I'd rather follow this adage: the best revenge is to live well. Depending on the intent of those who hurt you, some may be waiting in the background seeing how long you will stay down. Oh, no. Stay down? That's not in my DNA. I might stay down for a moment, but I will not stay down and live in despair. In this story of Paul's travels before he could get to his next place of ministry, he was stoned. The people who stoned him left him because they assumed incorrectly that Paul was dead. Nope! He got up, went to his destination, and ministered to other people. Now that's the best way to represent Christ!

Day 14

The Spirit of Fear

"For God has not given us a spirit of fear, but of power and of love and of a sound mind." (2 Timothy 1:7)

A few days after I started writing this book I had a terrible dream about being chased by demons. In the dream my parents were living in a city tenement with an outer door that could be bolted and a bedroom door that could not be locked. I could see the demons standing outside of the building and plotting their entry to the inside, but I felt secure that the locks would keep them out. They did not. With all of our strength and might, my parents and I were putting all of our body weight against the door to keep the demons out. I still remember my fear and breathlessness when I woke up. My first thought was that I could not write this book because of the spiritual warfare that would come as a result of sharing my story. But let me share about the beauty of God's plan. As I shared just a smidgeon of my story in the early days, there were men and women who could relate. When I began planning the release of the book, the response from friends was phenomenal and overwhelming. Many people do not want to have parts of their story scrutinized by the public eye, but many of them would set themselves and others free if they would confront their demons and tell their truth. Today as you reflect on the worst parts of your story, refuse to let the enemy and his demons keep you silent. Someone needs you to tell your story to give them the strength to tell theirs.

Day 15

Letting Go of Our Idols

Now the Lord said to Samuel, "How long will you mourn for Saul, seeing I have rejected him from reigning over Israel? Fill your horn with oil, and go; I am sending you to Jesse the Bethlehemite. For I have provided Myself a king among his sons." (1 Samuel 16:1)

At the beginning of 2018 I made two vows: to read the Bible more regularly and to write a daily blog. I decided to start in Isaiah, and I saw a trend while I was studying. The Israelites had a hard time letting go of idolatry. As I watched current news and just made observations in my life, it seems that many of us have made idols out of people and things.

I remember learning from my pastor that people can become idols in our lives. We look up to them, we idolize them, and dare I say we sometimes worship them. I know in my high school days there was a boy that I liked so much I told my friends that the sun set and rose at his command. Sounds foolish now, and although I never say things like that in my adult years, there have been people who captivated too much of my time and attention. The worst is that none of the people I placed in such high regard deserved it. And there was God as always waiting for me to turn my attention back to Him.

Maybe you are mourning over someone who left you. They didn't die, but they didn't choose you. Maybe you left someone because you recognized just how little they thought of you. I've been in both places. Leaving and being left, yet I mourned the loss. Thank God for a God who has designed a time and a day that He says, "No more!" No more mourning over something that He has removed from your life. No more mourning over what we see as a loss but God sees as a gain. The loss of a relationship does not indicate the end for us. In this verse God commanded his prophet to have an encounter with the one He had chosen all along. Do you know that God has already chosen you? I know that we often wait to be chosen, but we have already been chosen by an almighty God to be the vessel He uses to do mighty works in the earth. Daniel 11:32 says, "Those who do wickedly against the covenant he shall corrupt with flattery; but the people who know their God shall be strong, and carry out great exploits." You have already been chosen to carry out those great exploits. Don't let idolatry take your attention away from the call God has on your life.

Day 16

Forgiveness

"And forgive us our debts, as we forgive our debtors." (Matthew 6:12)

I was having a conversation with a group of women when I felt my temper rising, and I felt righteous indignation as they shared their stories of love gone wrong. I then talked to another friend about things going south in her relationship. By the time I got home I was feeling quite smug. I already knew that God was going to snatch me up quickly, and He did. I had been reading a book called "The Bait of Satan" by John Bevere as I wrote this book so that I could appropriately deal with letting offenses go, and I knew on this day I was going down the rabbit hole of not only being offended but holding grudges and being prideful. As I sat relaxing at the end of the day, an old memory of something I did released a flood of shame. Now the Bible refers to Satan as "the accuser of the brethren (Revelation 12:10), but I knew this wasn't Satan accusing me of a wretched past. This was Jesus. This was Jesus reminding me of the very thing that I regret the most was a sin for which He was crucified. I had been here before so this moment didn't surprise me. Anytime I become arrogant and judgmental, God will allow me to remember the very worst about myself. Instantly with just a few memories, it never fails that I hang my head in shame and tell God that I am sorry. I already repented for those sins I committed, but I tell Him how sorry I am that I placed myself in a position above someone else's sins. As much as I would like to think that life has humbled me, there is still more humbling I need to do. I have learned it is much better to humble myself before God does the humbling.

It can be easy to point out the faults in others while turning a blind eye to our own faults. By God's grace He does not allow me to stay in a finger pointing state very long because He and I both know my fingers should be folded in humble prayer instead.

Day 17

My Prayer For You

When it comes to brokenness, I have encountered two types of women. There are some who are broken and bitter, and there are others who are broken but better. When heartbreak comes, we have a choice. We can allow the heartbreak to break us forever and stay in a place of bitterness, or we can make peace with the heartbreak, move on, and become better.

Heavenly Father, I pray for my friends right now. I lift them up to You, along with all of their cares, concerns, and any area that is still broken. You are a merciful God, and I know that You care for us. You knew that this day would come before we were ever born. You said in Jeremiah that You knew us before we were formed in our mother's womb, so You knew us and every situation we would face. Father,

I know that You didn't design this situation to break us permanently. You are still working behind the scenes to grow, develop, and mature us. I pray in the name of Jesus' that You get the glory from this. I pray that only You and You alone will be glorified in my life and not the enemy. Thank You for trusting us to handle what only the toughest generals in Your kingdom can handle. We are the head and not the tail. We are above only and not beneath. You see us, You love us, and You have a plan for us even when things seem bad. Thank You in advance for raising us up to a new place in You. Thank You for keeping are hearts soft and compassionate and for keeping us from walking in bitterness. We praise You above our circumstances and trust You to work everything out on our behalf. In Jesus' name, Amen.

Day 18

Life After A Fall

"And the Lord said, 'Simon, Simon! Indeed, Satan has asked for you, that he may sift you as wheat. But I have prayed for you, that your faith should not fail; and when you have returned to Me, strengthen your brethren.'" (Luke 22:32)

In high school I thought that my most embarrassing moment was when I was racing through the hall in a pair of white pumps and fell flat on my bottom in front of the glass-encased office. I just knew that everyone had seen me fall, and if not, I knew that the people in the office were going to spread the word about what happened. No one came out of the office and commented, nor did I hear anything about the fall for the rest of the day. Moving onto my adult years, I had other embarrassing falls, but these were moral failures on my part. A bad decision here, and an indiscretion there. There were people who knew about these falls too, but instead of exposing me, they covered me. As I was preparing to write my year long blog, a very good friend prayed for me, and I wrote that blog openly and honestly knowing I was covered by her prayers. As I prepared to write this book, I had a certain level of fear because of the content and the fear of once again being exposed for my moral failure. But God! God sent another friend, a wonderful woman of God and prayer warrior, to let me know that I was still covered in prayer.

In this social media era we are bombarded by the mistakes that other people have made. Some people expose their own secrets, and others are unwillingly and/or unknowingly exposed. The reality is that all of us have fallen. Romans 3:23 reminds all of us of this. "For all have sinned and fall short of the glory of God." We can get caught up in our own shame and embarrassment and begin to think we are the only ones who failed. But what about other types of embarrassment? Maybe you were the recipient of someone else's indiscretion, and you are embarrassed because of what that person did. In both cases at some point we have to release the shame. Why? Because shame can silence us. Shame can also immobilize us to the point where we stop living fully. We have to get back up and move on. Yes, it happened. Yes, we may be embarrassed and sorry it happened. But let it go. Life will go on, and it is up to us to go on with it.

Day 19

God Says LIVE!!!

"And when I passed by you and saw you struggling in your own blood, I said to you in your blood, 'Live!' Yes, I said to you in your blood, 'Live!'" (Ezekiel 16:6)

During the writing of this book, two famous celebrities at the height of their careers committed suicide. I hadn't wrapped my mind around the death of the first celebrity when I heard the news about the second celebrity. I think it was fitting that I heard the news on a gospel radio station because in the discussion the radio host discussed the need for the church to be willing to talk about suicide, depression, and other mental health issues. Far too often we can wear a mask and pretend that we are okay when we are not. If we aren't pretending, maybe we are hiding.

In my first book I wrote about a group of people I call the walking wounded. Life has wounded their souls, and they are merely existing. Some people may go to work and fulfill their responsibilities, but they are not fully engaging in life with other people. I am in no ways minimizing anyone's pain. I have had my share of pain dealing with one calamity after another. But I took some advice from a very wise woman who is the reason I have survived these past three years. Her main advice to me was to change what I said to myself and to change my circle. As I was battling depression and anxiety, she encouraged me to surround myself with people who were not in the same place as I was. Let's reflect on that. If I'm depressed and anxious, do I need to only talk to people feeling the same way or should I reach out to people with the coping skills I was seeking? She asked me to change how I talked. In the morning rather than thinking I was going to be depressed or anxious, she asked me to identify reasons to be thankful. I spent a lot of time focusing on what was wrong with my life rather than what was going well. I consider it a blessing that my friend is a mental health professional who was able to help me navigate through the dark days, but I was willing to seek other professional help if I continued to experience more dark days than bright days.

I would love to end this one with my usual pep talk, but sometimes a pep talk just won't do it. I encourage you to be honest about where you are emotionally and take the steps that will best help you reach sound emotional health.

Day 20

Under Construction

"Being confident of this very thing, that He who has begun a good work in you will complete it until the day of Jesus Christ." (Philippians 1:6)

Just like I spent three years in equally bad relationships, I spent the same amount of time driving on a highway that was under construction. As soon as one construction project was completed, I would look up and more orange cones would appear! Are you serious? Are they really working on this highway again?! By the time my school year was complete the entire road had been uprooted and traffic rerouted so construction workers could rebuild the ramp yet one more time. Just thinking about it made my blood boil. Then I looked at my own life and compared it to those orange cones. For a long time I thought I would reach a point in life where all would be well and all of my problems would be fixed. Work would be great, my family would be doing well, and my personal life would be flourishing. Wouldn't you know it, life never worked out like that for me? Some aspect of my life was always under construction. I had money, but I also had health problems. I had my health, but I was struggling financially. Things were going well in every area except my personal life. When does it end? It doesn't. Just like we all have issues that need to be worked out, we ourselves are constantly under construction. One thing that writing this book taught me about myself is that there is always room for improvement—not just in my life's circumstances but also in the way I handle life's circumstances. My attitude is still under construction. My ability to forgive is under construction. The way I view adversity is under construction. Just like the highway hasn't been completed in three years, nor have I completed the work I need to do internally. And guess what? I won't be able to do it on my own. I had a moment when I wondered when was I going to get it all together, and I realized that I won't...at least not on this side of heaven. If I could get it all together on my own, I wouldn't need God's Spirit guiding me. I would only be standing up and telling a lie that I did the work. I have not done it, nor do I know when the work will be complete. But I am learning that it is okay to be under construction.

Day 21

What Does the Devil Have to Do with It?

"Now the serpent was more cunning than any beast of the field which the Lord God had made. And he said to the woman, "Has God indeed said, 'You shall not eat of every tree of the garden'?"

Now we address the elephant in the room: the devil. What does he have to do with any of this? I certainly won't insult your intelligence nor mine by saying "the devil made me do it." He certainly did not. What the devil does is present temptation, and we decide whether to give into the temptation or walk away. In addition, we can all be honest with ourselves and acknowledge if the people we deal with are God-sent or devil-sent. That sounds harsh, doesn't it? A long time ago an older person gave me some wise advice that I didn't heed. This senior saint said that when I meet people ask myself the following question—is this person going to bring me closer to God or take me further away? In both of my situations it is clear that both men took me further away from God and the calling He had on my life. I could look back now and bemoan that I'm not further along on my faith walk, or I can acknowledge that I allowed myself to be led astray; but either way I take full responsibility for the poor choices I made. Does the devil make us do anything? Not at all. Do we need to be aware of his tactics? Absolutely.

Day 22

What Does Love Have to do with It?

"And because lawlessness will abound, the love of many will grow cold." (Matthew 24:12)

As bizarre as it is to think about how we might have been tempted to do stupid things, it is more bizarre to know that all of us have done stupid things because of love. When I look back and think about what I did when I was young and in love, I can laugh about it and move on. The hard part is accepting the dumb things I did when I was old enough to know better. But that isn't the point of this portion of the book. This portion is a message to myself and anyone else who needs a message to not allow hurts from the past make your love for others grow cold. I certainly have felt my passionate heart grow dim out of the hurt, anger, and bitterness I felt towards someone I once loved. In my mind if that person hurt me, then I would just withhold love from others for as long as I deem necessary. In other words what some of us do is withhold love from people who had nothing to do with the original offense, yet we choose to hold them accountable for the wrongs done by someone else.

I thought of it like this. As a teacher my rules and the standards I have set have made some of my students angry. A student turns in a paper that is subpar, so I return it ungraded with the expectation for him/her to do the paper again. Most students redo the paper grudgingly, but a handful will glare at me and refuse to do anything. So what had the potential to be an "A" paper has now been thrown away and disregarded because the student can't get past the anger to redo the work. Who is now hurt by not doing the work? Not me because I have a college degree and a somewhat successful teaching career. Who is going to receive a zero? Not me because I am the one entering the grade.

I can admit that I have been known to have a spiteful "bite off my nose to spite my face" disposition, but I also have friends who will tell me the truth and not allow me to be an immature Christian by walking in bitterness. Is it hard to let things go? Of course, it is. Not only that, it is hard to let go of an offense that hurt you and then trust someone else again later down the road. This is about making an emotionally stable and spiritually mature choice to have healthy relationships by forgiving others and moving on. The alternative would be to remain spiteful and stunt the growth of potentially great relationships because of our inability to move on. I know that choosing to do what is spiritually mature isn't always easy, but it is what will move us to the place where we should be. Loving people after being hurt is extremely hard and a constant struggle for me, but it's something that I have to pray about and actively work on. Romans 5:5 is what initially got me to the place where I could even consider loving again because it taught me that I'm not loving people in my own strength. "Now hope does not disappoint, because the love of God has been poured out in our hearts by the Holy Spirit who was given to us." This verse was my reminder that I don't love others on my own strength because I can't. Oh, it's easy to love people who are kind and love me in return, but some people are difficult to love. Others, if I had my choice, I wouldn't extend myself to at all. But God! But the Holy Spirit! It's truly an exercise that I have to be consciously aware of and one that I choose to constantly perfect.

Day 23

Jealousy

"A sound heart is life to the body, but envy is rottenness to the bones." (Proverbs 14:30)

Just as it can be difficult to love people, we can also find ourselves jealous of other people, especially if they are in what we perceive as a healthy relationship and we are not. Notice I said perceive. At one time I was jealous of other people's relationships because I perceived that they were happy in love just because they were in a relationship. Then I realized that the grass isn't always greener in someone else's yard. Beyond being jealous of other people's relationships, I found myself being jealous of the fact that someone else was chosen, and I was not. Maybe you have questioned why someone was chosen and you were not. Maybe we judged the person who was chosen on their outward appearance and compared ourselves to him/her or we made assumptions about someone who has had terrible track record in regards to relationships yet he/she is in a somewhat healthy relationship. I've done it, and I didn't like where those negative thoughts led me. First it's the comparison, but if I'm not careful it becomes jealousy and then anger. One lesson that I wanted to learn in the process of healing was to be kind to myself, and it's hard to be kind to myself if I'm comparing myself to others and thinking that I don't measure up; and this is all based on thinking that I wasn't good enough to be chosen. Just like learning to forgive and to love others takes work, so does learning how to NOT be jealous of others. I had to learn that saying "I'm human" isn't a valid excuse. I've had to be honest with myself as soon as those thoughts enter my mind and address them. "No, I'm not so and so, but I don't have to be them to be valuable. I am not less than because I don't have a soulmate. I don't have to look like someone else to have value. I can be me and trust that I still have worth."

Day 24

Choose to Move

"This is the day the Lord has made; we will rejoice and be glad in it." (Psalm 118:24)

I've written abundantly about feelings, thoughts, and emotions, but I would be remiss if I didn't address movement. In my book Getting Fit For Life, I addressed the importance of physical activity, so when I faced this recent heartbreak I had to remain true to my mantra of moving no matter what. It was on a Wednesday that I was betrayed, and on Thursday I was in a dance class. I had the obligatory girls' night out dinner, but before dining with my friend I danced. One thing I have learned after losing and gaining weight most of my adult life is that movement is key to not only maintaining my physical health but my emotional health as well.

There would have been a time when I retreated to my couch with the remote and ice cream, but praise God, those days are over. Now…I move. Now…I dance. Now I don't allow anyone to stop me from being as healthy as possible. It is up to me to choose to eat healthy and exercise regularly no matter what obstacles come my way. Has life sometimes knocked me down? Of course! If I let it, life would have given me a death blow with the intent to see me buried, but I refuse to live defeated and unhealthy. Here are some questions to ask yourself. Are you moving? Do you engage in physical activities that challenge you both mentally and physically? How do you view the connection between physical movement and physical health? Maybe your answer to heartbreak is the couch, but can I challenge you to do something different? A funny thing happened after I started sharing about my heartbreak. The same people that I had already been exercising with began sharing with me their experiences with heartbreak. You know what I found? Comfort and closeness—camaradie and connection. The moments we spent dancing were not mere instances of misery loving company. Those moments were with people who understood my pain but like me refused to let pain define them. I challenge you to move beyond pain both emotionally and physically. This is a new day. Move and rejoice in it!

Day 25

Move Your Mind

Just like you have to choose to move your body to get physical exercise, you have to choose to move your mind from a negative space that is killing you emotionally and instead find the place of mental and emotional wholeness. I struggled for a long time trying to get my emotions under control. In fact, I used to get upset when wise people would tell me that I was in control of my emotions. What? How?!!! I had been ruled by my emotions for years so how could someone come along and tell me that I don't have to be ruled by them? I always equated my kind heart and love for others with my more erratic emotions and feelings and considerd myself to being overly emotional. It took time and maturity for me to separate the two types of emotions. Do I love people? Yes. Do I do things for others because of my love for them? Yes? But what about my negative emotions? As high in love as I can be, I can also be disappointed in people and that disappointment can turn into sadness, despair, anger, and other negative emotions. There is nothing wrong with being disappointed in people because it is bound to happen. I had to learn not to dwell in the negative emotions connected to that disappointment, and this is what gave me insight. I was reflecting on some people I have in my life, and in that group of people I could identify the ones who are always around supporting me and those who cannot be depended upon. As disappointed as I was at the actions of the ones who are not dependable, I thought about this. There have been times when I was not dependable, and in those times I just didn't have anything to give anyone. I realized that other people reach a place where they don't have anything left to give either. The best that I can do to maintain my peace of mind is to accept them for who they are, supportive or not, and to thank God for the ones who are present and helpful. Otherwise I would make myself and my heart sick worrying about people. There was a time when if my mind said, I want to be sad and disappointed today, then I would follow suit by listening to sad music and telling everyone who would listen that I was feeling down. Again, not a problem for a moment but definitely a problem if I stayed there for months. Proverbs 12:25 says, "Anxiety in the heart of man causes depression, but a good word makes it glad." Proverbs 17:22 says, "A merry heart does good, like medicine, but a broken spirit dries the bones." Both proverbs warn of the detrimental effect sadness has in a person's body, but they also remind us that sadness can be combated with a good word and a merry heart. In order to get to the place of joy, we have to choose to go in that direction. When disappointment or heartbreak comes, we have a choice. Cry and keep crying, or cry and dry our tears over time; but that is a decision that WE make.

Day 26

Facing The Worst Part of This

"Be anxious for nothing, but in everything by prayer and supplication, with thanksgiving, let your requests be made known to God; and the peace of God, which surpasses all understanding, will guard your hearts and minds through Christ Jesus." (Philippians 4:6-7)

On my road to recovery I learned a few things about myself and my thinking. I learned that I am anxious. I learned that in both cases I was anxious to have a relationship, and as a result I was willing to accept less than God's best for me. I learned that deep down I thought I could fix people. You would think that after spending three years with an alcoholic partner that I would have learned that people cannot be fixed by us. I accepted the womanizing behavior of the second person because underneath my confident exterior my lack of self-worth caused me to go along with it even though it was killing me internally. I thought eventually he would see worth in me and would stop being with other women. I was woefully wrong. I had a friend ask me one day if I liked fixing people; and I thought she was joking with me, but she made a valid point. There has been a pattern in the people I have chosen. I can't say that I purposely chose broken people, but I do think there is something to be said about the choices a broken person (me) makes. Looking back, I can see just how broken I was and why I thought it was okay to be with these people. The very first place of my brokenness was my divorce. By the time I met Adam, I thought I had recovered from the divorce, but there was still a part of me that was gun shy and afraid of a long-commitment. Years later when I met someone who was clear about not committing, I still stayed with him for three years with no commitment. One of the worst things about that fake relationship I created was that the brokenness I went into it with was multiplied by all of the betrayals and in-your-face behavior on his part. The last lesson I learned came from a wise woman of God who has taken me under her wing and is always there to give me timely words of wisdom. She said to me that only the Creator can fix people because they are His creation. Amen! Isn't that what I learned by writing this book? I was with someone who had the potential to

break me permanently and to take me off the path
God had for me. I chose to confront my brokenness
by diving in headfirst and writing this book. This
was me putting myself in the Potter's hands so I
could be remade. There is no one whom I can
remake in my hands, including myself. I can do
internal work by confronting my issues and dealing
with them head on, but changing certain parts of me
can only be done by God. I see where God is
working in my life—my attitude, my confidence,
my value, and the condition of my heart, which
leads me to the next point. Everything I just listed
are inward qualities, but they are manifested on the
outside. When we interact with broken people,
including ourselves, what we see outwardly is just a
manifestation of what is going on in the inside.
When I met these two people, I saw their outward
appearance, but I didn't really analyze why they
were behaving the way they were. The longer I
stayed, the longer their inward conditions affected
me, leaving me even more broken and in need of
God's help to rebuild. Like I said in the heading,
this was me facing the worst part of me and where I
was. It seems strange to quote Genesis 3:9 now, but
it's also a fitting way to close. "Then the Lord God
called Adam and said to him, 'Where are you?'"
When God asks us that, we have to answer honestly

in order to allow the full healing and rebuilding to begin.

Day 27

Still Singing

"He has put a new song in my mouth—praise to our God; many will see it and fear, and will trust in the Lord." (Psalm 40:3)

I was driving home from work listening to Mary J. Blige, and the lyrics to "Love Yourself" arrested me. Not only from the beauty of the words but because I knew the place from which she was singing. Real talk, when I heard about Mary J. Blige's latest divorce and how her ex was suing her for massive amounts of money, I was filled with rage on her behalf. But I never heard any stories about her doing the same. In fact every time I heard her music, she was still singing beautifully and powerfully. I looked up to God and said, how can this be? As much as life may hurt us, God has promised to put a new song in our hearts. The key is having a heart that is open to receiving that new song. At one point in my life the only music from me was discordant and harsh. Who was going to sing pleasant songs from a wounded heart? Certainly not me. But God! God's grace will lead you to a place where your heart can be healed no matter what has happened to you and produce a melody that will bring glory and honor to Him.

Day 28

The Power of Someone Else's Testimony

"And they overcame him by the blood of the Lamb and by the word of their testimony, and they did not love their lives to death." (Revelation 12:11)

Some people are afraid to share their testimonies of what they have overcome because they are afraid of other people's opinions. What if they see my flaws? What are they going to think of me when they find out I'm not perfect? I know that all of us know cognitively that we aren't perfect, but we do try to project at least a near perfect image to others. In all of this time spent recovering and living life in general I learned that it is people's stories of imperfection that best help me deal with my own struggles and imperfections. One thing that I learned by being a writer is to listen and appreciate other people's stories, particularly people's stories of conquering adversity. In one weekend I was able to spend time with three women who had some incredible stories of triumph. One woman survived domestic violence. The other survived cancer twice, and the third woman survived the murder of her daughter. As I was processing the end of a relationship and fighting the sadness, God allowed me to encounter these women in three different settings, and they blessed my soul in a tremendous way. The beauty of these three women is that two of them I knew for years before I knew what they survived. I had been friends with the cancer survivor and gleaning from her wisdom for several years before I knew she survived cancer twice at a young age. I knew her as friend, mother, and wise sage before I learned that surviving cancer formed much of her wisdom. My mother actually introduced me to the woman whose daughter was murdered, and I interacted with her for years in different settings before what she survived came up in a conversation with my mother. I stared back at my mother and thought about all of the funny conversations I had with this wonderful woman and was in awe of how God had healed her to the point that she could bring so much light everywhere she goes. Now the third woman is someone I met more recently. We met through a mutual friend and connected immediately. In the course of our conversation, I told her about the content of this book, supposing that such a spiritually strong woman could not relate to the topic. I was wrong! I told her the book was about two poor choices I made, and she responded by saying she had married two men who were wrong for her. One of her former husbands was physically abusive, while the other former husband abused drugs. She told me the length of both relationships and how she stayed in the second marriage longer because she figured that at least he wasn't beating her. In the short conversation we had she spoke many pearls of wisdom, but it was this one statement that impacted me the most. She told me that she had just seen her abusive ex-husband earlier in the week, and I gasped that she still had any kind of contact with him at all. She did not tell me the context of her running into him, but she did tell me that God had removed all of the pain of that marriage from her mind. She only gave me a glimpse of the horror of being beaten and kicked and traumatized, but she said when she thinks of those moments the physical and emotional pain connected to the abuse is gone. This let me know that God is a restorer. We can walk through the worst of the fire and still come out unscathed. I thank God for allowing me to meet these three women and for allowing me to hear their stories. They not only blessed me when I needed their testimonies the most, I know that they each have a gift to share with others. These women truly represent the power of God and what He can do with the worst of situations. I pray that when we go through our own fiery trials we will trust God to bring us out and be willing to share our testimonies with the next person who needs it.

Day 29

Beauty For Ashes

"The Spirit of the Lord God is upon Me, because the Lord has anointed Me
to preach good tidings to the poor; He has sent Me to heal the brokenhearted,
to proclaim liberty to the captives, and the opening of the prison to those who are bound; to proclaim the acceptable year of the Lord, and the day of vengeance of our God; to comfort all who mourn, to console those who mourn in Zion,
to give them beauty for ashes, the oil of joy for mourning, the garment of praise for the spirit of heaviness; that they may be called trees of righteousness,
the planting of the Lord, that He may be glorified." (Isaiah 61:1-3)

Isaiah 61 is a beautifully written, prophetic chapter about the ministry of Christ and what He would do for God's people. I don't remember the first time I read the chapter, but I do remember the first time I read it with a real revelation of the impact of Christ's ministry. I read verse one and wept. I continued to read down to the third verse and wept more. At the time I read it, I was well on my way to recovery and my heart was healing. I read these verses and began to believe in the exchange that God had for me. For all of my mess and my heartache, God was going to give me beauty for ashes. Correction, verse one says that Christ was anointed or empowered to carry out all of these promises written in Isaiah 61. Can you think of your lowest moment? I don't want to bring up awful memories, but we can't change what we won't confront. For me that phone call saying I'm leaving you for alcohol was my lowest moment. "I'm leaving you for alcohol. I'm choosing to drink myself into an early grave rather than be with you." Although these were not his exact words, these words summarize the context, and these are the words from which I thought I would never recover. If he had been there in person to kick me in the gut, they would have had a similar impact. But God! Isaiah wrote these words hundreds of years ago because God knew that a brokenhearted girl named Angie would need to read them. Not only that God had softened my heart to the point that I could receive them and internalize them forever. Beauty for ashes and the oil of joy for me. Wait? Does that say the garment of praise? Yes!!! No more wearing sadness and heaviness. Instead I'm putting on a garment of praise made just for me. I've been there in the worst moments, and I know it can seem like things will never get better; but I learned that these words of Isaiah are true. For all of those worst moments, there is an exchange that will happen. You may not be wearing your garment of praise yet, but there is one coming to you whenever you are ready to put it on.

Day 30

The Power of Purpose

"Before I formed you in the womb I knew you; before you were born I sanctified you; I ordained you a prophet to the nations." (Jeremiah 1:5)

Over the past six months I have been looking forward to celebrating my 20th year of being planted in and worshipping at my local church. Prior to joining this church, I rededicated my life to Christ at a women's conference and knew instantly that I needed to be a part of Calvary Revival Church because my spirit had truly been revived, and I needed to be connected to a ministry that focused on "building an overcoming church out of broken lives through the power of Jesus Christ", as stated in our vision statement. As I reflected and prepared for this momentous occasion in my life I couldn't help but think back to the highs and lows of my spiritual journey. As a new creation who was excited to be alive in Christ I had such high hopes of how my journey would follow that of a typical linear graph, and only go up as I rode the highs of my relationship with Christ. Somehow I missed the scriptures that said this life has troubles, so I was woefully disappointed when I had trouble in almost every area of my life, including my relationships. When I looked at the aftermath of these broken relationships, I almost lost sight of where I needed to return spiritually. God had a plan for me before the broken relationships, and He had one after they were over. Thankfully God reminded me of promises He made a long time ago, and He reminded me of the gifts He expected me to use. Yes, I had a broken life as stated in my church's vision statement, but I also had the power of Jesus Christ working inside of me. Problems have a way of shortening our vision. After all of these years at Calvary, I know the vision statement and have seen it in action; but there have been periods in my life that I became short-sighted and lost the ability to see my way past brokenness and actually moving forward. I've even said to God, "Lord, I messed up. Can You still use me? Are You sure You still want me to do what You called me to do?" The answer has always been YES. Jeremiah 29:11 says, "For I know the thoughts that I think toward you, says the Lord, thoughts of peace and not of evil, to give you a future and a hope." Most of us know that God has a plan for our lives. The key is believing that this promise applies to us even when things look bad. If I had believed that God had counted me out, this book would never have been written. I would not have shared my testimony with people I met in the aftermath. I would have said no to speaking engagements and opportunities to mentor young ladies. As painful as this chapter has been, it was for a bigger purpose and plan. This was God's plan and His purpose, and I had to say YES. Whatever He has planned for you to do, you still have to say YES.

Chapter 11

The Grand Finale

Take a deep breath and take one more ride with me. It was the Saturday after the last breakup, and I swore to myself that I was not going to share my story with a friend whom I was meeting for lunch. Within minutes I looked at her and knew I had to tell her the truth. She listened quietly, and after I spilled all the beans, she chose to spill hers.

Because I was brave enough to share my story, she was brave enough to share her story with me. We both knew that she had to include her story in this book. Listening to her that day was impactful, but later reading it on paper was mind blowing. I will say no more because I do believe these are the words I am to leave you with.

The Final Story – Written by Anonymous II

You are so much more than your worst mistake.

As I type those words my heart skips a beat. I feel a wave of shame come over me that says, "You are your worst mistake."

I slept with a married man. Not only did I sleep with him, but I devoured every part of him as if he were my own. As if God had made him specifically for me without realizing that God had made him for every part of me that I was trying to disconnect from.

I poured into him in ways I could never imagine. Moved mountains to get if even just a small smile. Put my heart on a wooden cutting board and watched as the pulse slowly died. Screamed out. Tried to save myself but I was gone.

He laid next to me. Night after night I felt the devil in my bed wrapped in chocolate skin with nice big hands that held the broken pieces I had never mended. I flirted with the idea of our future together while God fought for my soul.

I slept with a married man. A man who was married … me! I looked at that girl in the mirror every morning, and it was as if I looked past her. I hoped I would find the girl I used to know. The one who wasn't so desperate for the love of her father that she would stoop so low as to accept anything less than she deserved.

I looked past the girl in the mirror and hoped to find the girl who walked into rooms with dignity and pride. I think she stood in those rooms, because in my bathroom mirror she was nowhere to be found.

So I settled. For the half ass man who laid in my bed and the girl I saw in the bathroom. Day after day I put on makeup and took selfies to numb the feelings of pain and shame. I went after every goal you could possibly think of and believe it or not I actually achieved them.

I was carrying him. Him and his children. My home became his, my money became his, my body became his … but he never became mine. One day we were at a local restaurant and my card got declined after we ate (that was the first time anything like that had ever happened to me). I didn't blame him, but a huge part of me felt a sense of resentment. He didn't even flinch! Girl … as if this was a normal thing! There were signs that I truly believe Jesus was trying to show me at PF Changs! But like every other sign I pushed it aside. I loved harder. I decided I could fix things.

Ladies … WE CANNOT FIX A MAN!

I slept with a married man! I know I sound like a broken record but there is something about typing that out that drives shame out! There is something about sharing one of my deepest secrets with you that allows me to be just a little more free. FREEDOM. I think that is what we all ultimately want. Freedom from what our parents will think, freedom from what our boss will think, freedom from our own crazy mind, we just want to be free.

Parts of me felt free in that love affair. I felt like a rebel. I felt like I was doing something that was completely against our culture's norms, and I didn't care. But what I found … oh man!

What you choose as your source of freedom can also be your source of captivity. What you run to can quickly become what you want to run from. So choose wisely.

Choose.

Wisely.

A married man slept with me. I have to flip that around sometimes because parts of me feels like this was a one woman show, and I am the villain in your favorite Disney movie. But the truth is we all have a villain story and a victory story. He broke every promise he ever made to his Wife (even after he cheated before). He pieced together stories for me that felt like tomato soup on a cold winter day. I ate those stories up as if they were the last piece of substance I had, and I let him write his empty promises on my heart until they became stitched up, entwined with parts of my soul that I don't think I will meet until 20 years from now. I slept with the devil.

The devil slept with me. While he laid in my bed I felt a sense of hurt. I had let the little girl in me down. The little girl who dreamed of a man of her own. The little girl who wanted her man to propose to her with a Labrador retriever puppy who had a collar with the engagement ring attached (future hubby that's a yellow lab!). Here I was ruining that little girls dream sleeping with a man who couldn't even afford the dog's collar let alone deserve the woman that little girl had become.

As I reference my future husband I hear shame again! Loud and clear … "You really think God will bless you with a man?"

Shame is sneaky little thang I tell you. It will use the worst thing you have ever done and say to you that is WHO you are. It will make you completely forget whose you are!

I slept with a married man.

A married man slept with me.

And then he broke me. Down to pieces that I still don't recognize. Pulled me back into a world I thought I had left behind. Reminded me of why I had written off men in general. I wish I could tell you that I saw it coming. I wish I could say that there were signs. But to be completely honest while I was in it there weren't. Hindsight is always 20/20. But in the midst of it I was completely oblivious to how this man would completely shift my world.

It was a Friday night. We did the norm—leave home around 5pm to pick up the kids from daycare only this ride would be so different. We were arguing about my male friends. He proceeded to tell me that all of my male friends wanted to be with me and that I didn't know how to create boundaries. He asked, more so told me, to call each of my male friends in front of him and tell them that we could no longer be friends.

He was driving ... I actually like my life so I called!

One by one I felt embarrassment, resentment, anger, ALL OF THE FEELS.

They washed over me like the waves of the ocean flirt with the shore ever so softly pulling bits and pieces away. I got down to the last person that I was supposed to call, and my heart settled a little.

Then I got PETTY! Don't judge me ... Jesus is still working on me, Boo.

I asked him to see his phone and told him that I too had a list of people I wanted him to cut off. One of them being a woman he had cheated on his ex with prior to me (am I wrong for that ... congregation please tell me if I am wrong). I created my list and guess what ... he was NOT having it!

The tables had turned, and he didn't want to eat!

So let me rewind a little bit. I am from The Bronx. Where women like JLO and Cardi B are produced so you can understand when I tell you that I have the capability of crazy!

I went off! And my request became demands. He had made me go through an embarrassing moment and cut off my friends now it was time for him to do the same. (Disclaimer: I have matured since this happened and I believe that given the opportunity I would handle this differently.)

This escalated quickly.

He said he wasn't going to call anyone, and I kept demanding that he make the phone calls. Once we picked up his kids I quieted down (I have a thing with acting crazy in front of kids). The tone of my voice quickly changed, but my words were probably just as angry. I asked that we continue the conversation when we got home, but he had to prove his point so he continued. I felt my skin crawling in the only way skin crawls when it is trying to remove your body from the current location … disassociation. Numbing. Choose the word you would like—I felt it.

I quickly tried to get out of the car and he zoomed off to get onto the nearest highway, and it was at that moment that I realized *this man did not love me*. Hell, I wonder if he even loved his kids (they were in the car remember). My emotions flooded my heart to the point where I was drowning. I was drowning in my own body no water in the distance, but a life jacket clearly needed. I heard the voice of the man from my last abusive relationship "no one will ever love you" and I cringed. I felt the punch to my face that left broken front window shields and my earrings bent and I just drifted. Was I really here again? Had I come this far only to sink? I thought I had built a boat as tough as the Titanic, but let's face it even the Titanic wasn't ready for what hit it.

I would like to take a moment to say that this would have been the time to walk away! I hear you. But ya girl is stubborn.

We made it home that night. Conversation was casual like nothing ever happened. I was used to acting. Ordered pizza. Put the kids to sleep and called it a night. I woke up the next morning. Picked out my favorite outfit and decorated my face. I say decorate because makeup is more for a cover up and at this point I was trying to change the whole entire person I was looking at. I cooked some breakfast, you know to make sure his kids ate some food, got my things and left for the day.

My hopes ... when I got home he would be gone.

Who am I kidding?

He had it made!

Food

Internet

Sex

That man wasn't going nowhere!

At least not permanently or physically.

But on his phone ... Chile, he had been all over the world up in the DMs getting pictures I would prefer to unsee because ewww.

Ladies please keep it classy. Naked pictures are not cool ... Especially if he ain't your hubby or if you don't have clean clothes on. STOP IT!

That night we talked, and I listened to his now sour tomato soup story. I ate it a little more reluctantly this time, but I finished my food. We played around with the kids, pillow fights are always a good way to smack someone upside the head without really hurting them and we chilled. I thought to myself we will be good ...

LIES!

ALL LIES!

A few moments later his phone lit up. I could see that we had not fully resolved the issues by the look in his eyes. I kindly ask to see his phone and he agreed. Not even 2 sec (I am not lying, girl) I find naked pictures from a woman. I felt nothing, and yet I felt everything. It was like a draining feeling that didn't leave me feeling empty it just left me as I was.

I tossed the phone at his belly and simply said "I'm done."

What happened next is probably the most difficult thing for me to write. I had survived domestic violence before. I now worked with women who were in these situations, and I thought I would NEVER have to go through this again.

He picked his Iphone 7 plus up and threw the phone at my face. He aimed the phone at my face. I could see it in his eyes. It was intentional. He wanted me to understand that he had more power. (BTW IPhones are a weapon! That thing felt like a 9mm glock was hitting my head). I felt my eye swelling. I couldn't see the room clearly. I felt lightheaded and I was so confused. My brain immediately kicked into cover up so I went to the freezer to find a frozen veggie bag to put on my face and I cringed. My eye was throbbing! My head was spinning. And he … he was trying to prove his innocence. I remember him asking me to look at a message between him and said woman … but I couldn't open my eyes.

Till this day he has not apologized.

I spent the next two weeks trying to figure out ways to hide the bruise. Finding the right foundation. Googling home remedies for swelling and if I can keep it totally 100 with you I think that was the most heartbreaking.

Hiding.

I had been hiding this whole relationship from some of the most important people in my life. Because of shame. And now … now I was forced to hide the bruises that this relationship had left. Every morning for the next two weeks I used my foundation brush to put concealer and then foundation over the bruise. As the hairs on the expensive makeup brush touched my skin I squinted. It hurt to cover up, and it hurt to look at it.

Isn't that so ironic?

The bruise on my eye reminded me so vividly of the relationship as a whole … It hurt to cover up and it hurt to look at it.

That bruise healed about two weeks after the incident.

Two weeks of weak smiles because cheek bones hurt after your face is smacked.

Two weeks of seclusion because shame won't allow you to talk to anyone about it.

Two weeks of avoiding facetime calls from your mother because you don't want her to worry.

Two weeks of figuring why …

Pivot.

Jenny Blake says, "The only move that matters is your next one."

Next move:

At the time I didn't know my next move … my world felt out of place. I felt darkness. My heart was barely keeping up with the other parts of my body. I became numb. Maybe I am still numb. Maybe as you are reading this I am becoming less numb.

I decided.

Side note: One of the most important lessons I have learned in my short time on this earth is that DECISION is everything.

I decided that I was going to put myself back together.

That sounds cliché and is way easier said than done.

Have you ever opened a puzzle box and realized that there was a piece missing?

It is so freaking ANNOYING!

Like WHY???

That is what putting me back together felt like … like missing puzzle pieces and pieces that didn't even belong. For someone who already dealt with dysfunction and depression, talk about OVERLOAD. I was done. I felt defeated. He had won.

Isaiah 53:5 "But He was wounded for our transgressions, He was bruised for our iniquities; the chastisement for our peace was upon Him, and by his stripes we are healed."

In another version it says, *"He was beaten so we could be whole"*

I sat on my couch as I heard God speak to me through this scripture. He said I already took care of this. You do not need to keep picking at this wound because I have already taken the heat for it. I heard him ask me … do you want to be whole?

I have realized that you can be holy and not be whole. And God did not send His only Son to die for us to ACT holy; it says right in the word that he sent His Son so we could be whole!

I felt God saying to me "this show you been keeping up ... it looks good, but you are the main act and I can't perform if you are not willing to give up that spot."

The Message:

I tried so hard to fix this on my own. To fix the relationship, to fix the person, to make sure other people didn't think of me any type of way, to put myself back together and all the while God just wanted me to let Him do His part.

Surrender.

It sounds nice but ooooohhhhh it is one of the hardest things I have done. One of the hardest things I continue to strive toward every day. To really let go and let God. To allow God to come into my heart and really work on the stories I had been replaying in my head. I don't know about you, but I have trust issues. Surrendering to anything that is out of my control is a big NO NO. I have walls so high that 7 times around wouldn't even break through the wall covering the wall. Are you copying? So for God to tell me ... give me that! Give me that shame. Give me that embarrassment. Give me that pain and resentment.

GIVE

ME

THAT

Uh No !!!

But God doesn't really take to no … He is persistent.

Like a toddler.

Who wants Oreo cookies.

And sees them at the top of the fridge.

Like that.

A few days go by and I hear God say to me … let me cover these wounds so that you may be whole. And I thought to myself wounded to wholeness, that would be how God works. I sat down … (my living room floor is the most comfortable for things like this) and I cried. I cried so hard that I felt like I needed to gasp for air. I cried until I no longer knew what I was crying for.

The next few weeks I decided to be still. Not stand still, but BE still. I worked. Finished projects. Started new ones. But I acquired a stillness in me and I just processed. Personal development is so annoying, y'all! Like it's really necessary but so annoying. I cried in the middle of the day for no reason. I wrote about things that happened to me when I was 11 and 13. I dug deep into my daddy issues (not deep enough though) and I just processed.

Side note: I think a lot of us want to avoid the process, but we want to receive the promises of God and what I have learned is that you cannot have one without the other. It's like PB&J.

Where is she now (Like high school alumni parties have):

I am still healing. God is still working. There are parts of that love affair - if we can still call it that - that I will hold close by to my heart and parts that I have chosen to bury. I have accepted Grace so I am able to fully give it. I forgive that man for whatever led him to do what he did to me. I forgive myself for whatever led me to think that I deserved so little.

What I hope you take from this:

You can be broken and still shine bright.

You can actually be broken and put yourself back together again and then be broken again.

You can fall short and still stand tall.

You deserve the very best this world has to offer.

You are so freaking amazing!

You have magic inside of you … like straight magic.

You are so much more than your worst mistake.

So am I.

Made in the USA
Middletown, DE
10 June 2019